Pictorial representation of the farm.

"Now be a good Aunt…!"

Memories of My Family & of a Pioneering Life
and a Childhood in Southern Rhodesia

By
Philip Greenhow

A Bright Pen Book

British Library Cataloguing Publication Data.
A catalogue record for this book is available from the British Library

ISBN 978-0-7552-1592-8

Authors OnLine Ltd
19 The Cinques
Gamlingay, Sandy
Bedfordshire SG19 3NU
England

This book is also available in e-book format, details of which are available at www.authorsonline.co.uk

Dedication

This book is dedicated to my mother, who imbued me from an early age with a love of poetry and literature, and who educated me at home until the age of eight . Thereafter she brought me up when she saw me with love and pragmatism, and taught me how fortunate it is, when dealing with adversity, to be able to do so with a sense of humour.

The author, with Whiskey O'Growler and pet duiker.

Contents

Chapter Number   Heading

List of Illustrations

Introduction

An autobiography, it has been said, is a landscape with figures.

The landscape in this book is in Southern Rhodesia; the figures in it are mainly those of my family.

Southern Rhodesia is now a country which no longer exists; the land is now called Zimbabwe, and it is a sad country. This book is not about Zimbabwe, and the story is not all sad.

For half a century there was peace in Southern Rhodesia. Peace is a quality to be valued, even if it is accompanied by a certain lack of freedom, or prosperity, or if making a living is hard. My parents were part of that time; they also had to struggle for a better life. Neither of them was brought up to be pioneer; my father was the son of a clergyman, my mother was the daughter of a doctor. Each faced their life in Rhodesia in the best way they knew.

Africa is a beautiful country, but a harsh one. Africa has no use for art, or for duty, laughter or other qualities peculiar to the English, but continues on its own mysterious way, inscrutable and indifferent.

My father chose to settle there; my mother arrived almost by accident. My father made a farm where previously there had been nothing but open bush , as unchanged as it had been since Adam and Eve first met. My mother stoically stayed for twenty five years, but always pining for England, her home sickness often expressed in her letters to her favorite Aunt, who, God bless her, kept them.

My father died in Africa. My mother returned to England to recover, to re-join some of the family she had known as a child, and to enjoy the autumn of her life.

The English who went out to Rhodesia in the early days did not have an easy life, and those who settled there were mostly not, like some who were sent to Kenya, spoilt or decadent. Rhodesians worked hard, and faced their harsh and lonely lives with endurance, often assisted by a good sense of humour.

Chapter 1. Introducing the Aunt. My mother's childhood.

"My Dearest Auntie Flo, Now be a good aunt and write me a line. I haven't heard from you for ages, and I want to know how you all are…"

So wrote my mother from Africa in the early 1930s. The feeling of loneliness, and her heartfelt need of news from 'home' - she always referred to England as 'home' – are evident from this and many other letters from her which she wrote to her favorite aunt at this time. She had married my father a year or two before she wrote it, and was living on the farm he had created out of virgin veldt in Southern Rhodesia. The address at the head of her letter, which was 'Private Bag 104C, Salisbury', gives no hint of the remoteness of that farm then. Private Bag 104 C was in fact a canvas bag into which their mail was sorted in Salisbury, the capital city of the colony, to be put on a train once a week from whence it was thrown off onto a dusty little railway halt which was over one hundred miles away. This halt had been given the name 'Baddeley Siding', a name much too grand for its squalid appearance.

My mother, as you will find, was not the sort of woman most people would have considered to be " the Pioneering Sort". Nevertheless, she had a courage all her own. Neither had my father, whom you will meet shortly, any farming background. His father had been a parson in a small village in Dorset. So, how did they find themselves so far from England, in a sparsely populated part of Africa, both trying to create a new life, a good English way of life of course, against such unknown odds? For Africa, however alluring she looks on her surface, is inwardly indifferent to the puny efforts of man, particularly those from softer countries such as England.

Aunt Flo, to whom my mother was writing, was one of five sisters with the surname of Peach. Orphaned early, all five were brought up by a Christian and loving aunt, and, when they were grown up, three of them set up house together in Leavesden. Here they did good works, played tennis, and soon became known in the neighbourhood as the " three beautiful Miss Peaches." (I suspect the word 'Miss' was sometimes omitted in this description by local young men). There is a picture of the three of them on the next page. The youngest sister, my grandmother Emily, was the fairest of them all, and was known as 'Zem'.

The Three Miss Peaches, Lin, Flo' ('Aunt Flo') and Zem.

The sisters did not remain spinsters long, the local press describing three "fashionable weddings" in a short space of years. Cuttings pasted in Zem's album contained descriptions of each of these in succession, all with remarkable similarities. At each there was the same opening hymn, 'Oh Father All Creating', and after each a certain Mr. Pusey provided "a carriage and pair for the bridal couple." Many of the same guests appeared at each reception. This was not surprising since two male cousins married two of the Peach sisters and the third sister's groom was a doctor known to the other two. So the weddings provided for a very tight family circle later.

The third wedding to take place in Leavesden Church was that between Emily Peach, my grand-mother, and my grandfather, Dr. Cecil Powell. One press account recounts that:-

"...the Doctor had a most pleasant surprise on the way to his wedding, for the whole of the children from the schools were there with their officers to give him a send-off. The horses slowed down and the school band, under the direction of Bandmaster Woodman, marched in front playing a wedding march, the boys and girls all following behind and waving their handkerchiefs with great glee..."

What a happy picture, and how different to the wedding of my mother in 1930, when alas no relatives and few friends would be present.

My mother was born on 15th February 1902, thankfully missing by just one year being a 'Victorian'. She was christened Cicely, and was later known to her family and friends as "Cissie". Her brother Christopher was born one year later, to be followed after a gap of seven years which would later prove of significance, by another brother, Sam.

"We dearly loved our beautiful mother", wrote Cissie in her memoirs later, "who possessed in full the Peach charm present in all the sisters. They all had their own special brand of humour and shared a love of animals. In addition they all thought quite a lot of themselves! Mummy was nervy, but more methodical and business-like than Daddy. She made delicious jam, bottled fruit and played the piano with skill and feeling. On Sunday evenings she would sit down at it and we would all gather round and sing, nursery rhymes and hymns to start with – we each had our favourite – and later from the Student's Songbook of British Ballads or the Plantation Songbook:-

"Shine, shine Moon,
One last dance with Dinah, dear..."

At Calverton House in Stony Stratford where they lived, Zem had her own storeroom where she kept tea, sugar, jam etc., which was rationed out each week to Cook. Zem carried around a key basket with a notebook always in it, always being very methodical.

Doctor Powell had, according to legend, established his excellent reputation in the practise very soon after he had arrived. A baby, purple in the face and choking, was brought in to him in a great flurry. "Doctor, doctor, 'ee's 'aving a fit", shrilled the distraught mother. " Nonsense"! said the forthright doctor, who seized it by the heels and clapped it heartily on its' back. There was a tinkle as sixpence dropped from the baby's gullet onto the hard floor. "He'll be as right as rain now", said the good doctor, handing it back to its relieved mother together with the coin from the floor, and sure enough it thrived thereafter.

Calverton House, where my mother spent most of her childhood, looked down across its own lawns and meadow to the river Ouse. A bathing area was created in the river by cutting the weed, and there the doctor's children received their first swimming lessons, and later swam with cousins and friends. Swimming lessons were given by Doctor Powell. His methods were simple. He tied one end of a rope to the end of an oar and the other end round the child's waist. The child was then suspended in the water, while he walked up and down along the bank, often talking to a friend and disregarding the frequent spluttering and choking beneath him as he did so. He had been a good swimmer himself while at Cambridge – I still have a biscuit barrel he won there for 'plunging fifty five yards' – so thought little of the difficulties. "... So we all learnt very quickly", said my mother later. Since he also took all his children out riding from a very early age

- Christopher went out hunting from the age of seven - I am not surprised Zem was occasionally a little "nervy".

The house had fine herbaceous borders in front tendered by Zem, and large kitchen gardens in which were grown, in addition to the usual vegetables, asparagus, rhubarb and sea kale, the latter being forced in straw in large earthenware containers. Two gardeners were employed. There were numerous fruit and walnut trees. Walnuts, once harvested, were barrrowed in sacks to a cellar to be stored in damp sand, ready for use over winter.

Sunday lunch always began with a sirloin of beef, expertly carved by Dr. Powell, a Surgeon as well as a Physician. At the end of the meal he liked to relax with a glass of port. If there were young cousins staying he delighted in entertaining them with gory stories of medical life, which were embroidered specially for them. My cousin Phil recalled being given a description of how he had carried out the amputation of an old lady's leg in her cottage. The cottage was so small that her bed needed to be pushed up to the bedroom door to allow Dr. Powell to operate from outside the bedroom on the landing. "And then", said Phil with glee, "he took a banana and showed us how!"

When the boys grew older they played jokes on the gardeners and the maid, Olive. One joke was ingenious, but cruel. One Halloween a fearsome looking 'Guy' was prepared well before the forthcoming fifth of November. It was placed one night in an armchair in the ill-lit patient's waiting room, half- covered with a rug. Olive, having been 'primed' earlier with ghoulish stories of the witches, wizards and other things which go 'bump' in the night during Halloween, was then sent to the waiting room to stoke up the fire. She speedily arrived, after discovering this horrible object, back in the kitchen, where she had to be comforted by Cook. Meanwhile young Sam was dressed in the Guy's clothes and hidden under the rug in the same armchair. Olive was told that the fire must now nearly be out and really should be stoked. While she was doing this, Sam arose from the chair behind her with an eldritch screech and flung out his arms. Olive, poor lass, fled in hysterics. Everyone who was ' in the know ' thought this joke a great success except Olive and Cook, who plotted their own revenge later.

At Christmas- time a succession of carol singers, bands and hand-bell ringers would call to perform, and to be fortified afterwards. There was also an annual Fair on the Green, when steam driven roundabouts and swings operated to loud and cheerful tunes, and kept the whole town awake late. There were even performing bears which appeared from time to time, to perform disconsolate little jigs outside the back door. These were discouraged by Zem, who loved animals. One day a bear was reported as having escaped in the locality. This gave Olive her chance. She and Cook regaled Sam with stories of the frightful things bears did to little boys whom they came across in their wanderings. Sam refused to go to bed thereafter unless his bedroom window was firmly closed beforehand and a search made under his bed , and this state of affairs continued until the bear was reported as recaptured.

By 1913, Aunts Flo, Lin and Fan all had children of similar ages to Zem's. Of these, one later became an Admiral, and two were knighted, but at this time they were all growing up and frequently staying at Calverton House, swimming, boating and riding , or playing tennis or charades. It was a happy time, only broken by the outbreak of the First World War.

Chapter 2. My father's time in the first World War.

When the First World War began, my father Maurice Greenhow was one of the first volunteers. He had just left Lancing College, and was cramming for university. No doubt to the dismay of his parents, he enlisted as a private, but was soon selected for officer training, and sent to the Royal Military College, Sandhurst. On leaving he joined the West Yorkshire Regiment (both his father and his grandfather were from that county) and from thence volunteered for the Royal Flying Corps.

Maurice Greenhow on leaving Sandhurst.

In 1915 he was posted to France as an Observer. The R.F.C. was in its infancy, and its aircraft were primitive and mainly used for observation purposes. Most aeroplanes had two seats, and two sets of wings held together by struts and wires. The Observer was in command and sat in front. Little training was given to the army officers sent out as observers. Maurice's younger brother, who was killed as an observer in 1917, had only fourteen hours flying time logged when he followed his elder brother out to France in 1916; during those fourteen hours he suffered 3 crashes, each due to a 'dud' engine.

The aircraft in which Maurice found himself flying was called the 'B.E. 2C'. Cecil Lewis, in his classic book about flying in the R.F.C., 'Sagittarius Rising', says of it:-

"If there was ever an aircraft unsuitable for active service it was the B.E. 2C. The pilot sat slightly aft of the main planes and had a fair view above and below except where the main planes obscured the ground forward, but the observer who sat in front could see virtually nothing, for he was wedged in the small center section with one plane above and another below, and bracing wires all round. He carried a gun for defence, but he could not fire forward because of the propeller. The synchronizing- gear which enabled a machine gun to fire through a whirling propeller and still miss the blades had not yet been perfected by the British. To the rear the center section, struts, wires and tail- plane of the aircraft all cramped the observer's style."

By 1915 the German air force had developed aircraft with machine guns which could fire through the propeller at the front.

On 25th September, 1915 the squadron in which Maurice was serving was only just giving its aircrew a Lewis gun with which to defend themselves; up until then the only weapon carried was a revolver given to the pilot. This is apparent because on that day Second Lieutenant Greenhow was ordered to drop a bomb on a railway junction near Douai; he having been selected because he was the only Observer available who had been instructed how to use this weapon. To do this in his aircraft, he had to stand up in the cockpit, turn round and rest the gun on the top plane. This gave him a restricted field of fire, above and to the rear only.

My father was a taciturn man, and never spoke about the action. It was only when sorting old papers after his death that I came upon his account of what followed on that day. It was written in pencil shortly after the event on a rough piece of paper. Here it is:-

"...Started at 7 a.m. Fired at by machinegun after crossing trenches. Bullet later found in engine sump. Dropped bomb - terrific air bump - climbed, and flew West. Two Hun machines, 1 dope coloured, 1 light blue appeared. One kept pace left, the second opened out, circled to right rear, and waited until first machine fired. No. 2 then attacked, both of us fired a drum - no results. No. 2 banked away. No. 1 attacked, charging head on.

Suddenly went into a spinning nosedive, completely out of control. Oil everywhere, eyes, hair, neck, goggles. Turned round and faced the sky. Pilot threw his revolver overboard - watched it falling. Waited for him to pull her out - nothing happened. Thought we were for it and waited for the crash. Sudden silence - engine switched off and we landed, bumping heavily over plough furrows. Got out badly wounded pilot with help of peasant, ran back to fire the machine. Put my foot on the step, but as I did so, Hun officer appeared, revolver in hand, polite but very gruff. Then the crowd, followed by eight cavalry at a gallop. First Hun machine landed, then second. All shook hands and saluted.

"C'est la guerre," said No. 1.

My pilot had both legs smashed, 1 below and 1 above the knee, and a bullet in the groin. First Aid valise produced, and he was carefully bandaged, just conscious at the time. Red Cross Wagon with two horses arrived with brandy and lukewarm coffee. We were then taken across country with a mounted escort to a village. My pilot, Second Lieutenant Washington, was later reported as 'died of wounds'. The German pilot said of my aircraft:-

"The Germans would not have such a machine near the lines."

My father believed he was shot down by the famous German ace, Max Immelman, the pilot who invented the manoeuvre known as the 'Immelman Roll'. The reason for both German pilots landing in the same field was that they wished to establish which of them had been successful. A biography of Immelman, written after his death, does record that his third victim was shot down on the 25th September, 1915.

The German pilots subsequently dined Second Lieutenant Greenhow in their mess.

He was then put in a French cell in solitary confinement for eighteen days. During this time the Germans sent in two meals a day for him, and he made two friends. These were mice; one became so tame it would eat from his hand. I have a picture of the cell drawn in pencil on the inside of a cigarette carton.

"My cell as sketched by me while doing 18 days solitary confinement at St. Quentin, 15th September onwards. 3 plank bed. 2 meals per day. Company - 2 mice (tamed). Drawn on inside of cigarette carton."

For the rest of the war he was a prisoner. His mother learnt that he was still alive from the American Express Bank of America. They wrote to her informing her that they had cashed a cheque for £4 for Second Lieutenant M.W. Greenhow at their Berlin Branch, adding that they were aware that such news was often the first that relatives received that their sons were still alive. The United States had not in 1915 declared war on Germany.

In 1918 he was repatriated to Holland, and from thence to England. His possessions were few - some photographs and programs of theatrical productions put on by the prisoners, a few tin coins produced for use in the camps by the Germans and, most prized, a Royal Straight Flush in Spades, the highest possible hand in the game of Poker, framed, glazed and the cards signed by the officers playing in the game when Maurice won it.

The war ended, and he rejoined his regiment. But he had no friends left in the regiment, peace time soldiering did not appeal, and a large army was no longer required by an impoverished country. He started to look for a new career.

On 30th May, 1920 he wrote to his mother:-

"...I have just found a description of farm life in Rhodesia. If you buy the 'Empire' number of the Field, you will see all about it. It gives the bright side and the disadvantages, so I think is accurate. It appears to me to be a more suitable country than Australia - more variety of stuff can be produced, less capital is needed, and lastly it is not so far away from England. Do you think you would be able to put up some capital about next autumn without inconvenience?"

"Rhodesia, the Land of Opportunity" is the heading of the article in the 'Field' dated 29th May, 1920 which caught my father's eye and changed his life. It begins by giving a short history of the colony since it had been founded in 1890 by Cecil Rhodes' British South Africa Company, and ends, "those 30 years have been far from un-chequered, and the early history is one of conflict with native insurgents but Rhodesia has survived successfully those birth pangs, now possesses a contented and prosperous native population, and is free to continue development as a mineral bearing and farming community. Later in the article the prospects for cattle ranching, and the growing of maize, tobacco and citrus fruits are considered, together with the availability of railways, hospitals and schools.

"Early rain appears in October and lasts intermittently until the beginning of April," it reports and,

" from May to September the sun shines from a blue sky. Self - reliance, energy and doggedness are the characteristics most demanded, and the Empire Builder who chooses Rhodesia would be ill advised to start without adequate capital. As to his baggage, the less the better, but amongst it should be a medical kit including permanganate of potash, quinine, and sticking plaster, together with a mosquito net, a camp bed and a .303 rifle."

Much of the advice in that article was sound. The British, whatever their faults, had established law and order in a country where previously it had not existed. Thereafter the Mashona tribes were no longer threatened by their warlike neighbours to the South, the Matabele. When I was a child, many of the kopjies still showed the remains of stone fortifications which had been constructed before the British arrived so the local population could take refuge in them when the Matabele were on the war path. There was a steep- sided little kopjie only a quarter of a mile from the farmhouse on my father's farm which had only one way up to the summit, up a narrow cleft. A doorway so low that one was forced to crawl to get through it, and which therefore could easily be defended, had been built with stones across the bottom of this cleft. The Mashona had done this so they could take refuge there whenever the Matabele were in the vicinity, looking for cattle and women. A photograph of this doorway, with an Irish terrier sitting in it gives an idea of its size.

The fortified entrance to the Fort Rock.

But the article in the 'Field' had a purpose. Britain still had an Empire in 1920, and no shame was felt in encouraging its young men to expand or improve it. Those who already farmed in Rhodesia and knew about the droughts would have given a wry smile at the description of the rainfall as being 'intermittent', and if

21

the only tropical disease to affect man or beast had been malaria life would have proved a lot easier. So the article rather glossed over the difficulties that would be met. But there were many unemployed in England, so the Field probably intended to encourage emigration to the undeveloped colonies. A more thoughtful warning about the loneliness of life there might have been given than that a settler required 'doggedness' however.

But for a young man who had been confined in overcrowded conditions for over three years, and who had on release when peace was declared found that the description of England as a "land fit for heroes" was far from the truth, the description of a new country where self- reliance and honest hard work could extend the Empire and where, moreover, the sun shone from a cloudless blue sky for half the year, the description must have seemed irresistible. There before him lay a prospect of space, freedom and a new life.

Chapter 3 My mother's upbringing and the death of her parents

The outbreak of war disrupted the happy family life in Calverton House. The partners tossed up to see who would enlist, and it was Doctor Powell who went off to the Front in the Royal Army Medical Corps. As he was over age, he was allowed to enlist on a yearly basis.

Cissie was sent to boarding school. It was not a good school, and when Zem went to see her there during an outbreak of whooping cough she was so horrified by the conditions that she withdrew her daughter immediately. For a while thereafter, Cisssie had lessons at home. Piano lessons from her mother were not a success. Zem was musical, with a medal from the Royal Academy of Music, but Cissie was not. But drawing lessons were a joy , and it soon became apparent that Cissie had great talent in this respect. In due course she went to a smaller and better school run by a Scots Head Mistress, where only the food was poor. This was because the German submarine blockade caused food shortages and rationing. The Head Mistress was a brilliant teacher of English Literature and of the King James Bible; both became a love of Cissie's thereafter.

Cissie also had a talent for making friends, and here she made a lifelong and loyal one in Nancy Gee, whom she loved and fought with for the rest of her life. She also started another lifelong pastime, the composition of rhyming verses, usually triggered by an unusual name. The first of these concerned their unfortunate History Mistress:-

We knew Miss Leas

Had fleas

When she asked for the keys

Of the cupboard

Where the Keatings was kept.

(Keatings was the name of a well- known insect powder).

Cissie left school with Honours in Drawing, English Literature and Divinity, all subjects which she enjoyed in later life, and a much treasured book of Keats' poems. The latter was not a prize, but a gift to her inscribed, 'with love from all the inmates of the Pink Room'. One of the inmates was Nancy Gee; all the inmates signed it.

Meanwhile the Practice in Stony Stratford was going to pieces, since the patients missed Doctor Powell and Zem was becoming 'nervy'. So after two years at the Front, Doctor Powell was permitted to return, and it was his partner's turn to do Army service.

In 1917 tragedy struck where least expected. A letter from Zem foretold it, the chatty beginning of the letter disguising shattering news in its second paragraph:-

"My dearest Flo,

Yours to hand this morning - so glad to hear you had a good time at Oundle. I had faint hopes of seeing you, as I knew you would want to be back with Phil as soon as possible. How splendidly he's done!

Had you come, it would only have been to find me sounding like a slobbering idiot. Suddenly yesterday afternoon I was seized with facial paralysis. Without the slightest warning, (and with friends to tea), I found to my great alarm that I could not manage my lips or speak clearly. It was very frightening, I can assure you, and of course I thought I had had some kind of stroke or heart attack. But directly Cecil saw me he pronounced it to be facial paralysis, which comes on in twenty four hours sometimes. He hopes to get me right in a week's time, but it is most aggravating and makes me feel such a fool.

Zem."

…"right in a week's time"! Oh, Doctor Powell, what a reassuring professional! And what a white lie! Zem died of a brain tumour only a few weeks later, leaving her family in the greatest misery. A last letter to her daughter was kept by her for the rest of her life.

"Cissie,

This is not going to be a sentimental letter - I could not write what I feel - it is so much. Let me go to business matters. The little I have to will as I like I have left to you because, as I tell the boys, they can get along so more easily than a girl can. Try and understand money matters when you come of age. Dads will explain how things stand. Go to Aunt Flo any time you would have come to me about things, darling. She looks on things from the same stand point as I do, and I love and respect her.

God bless you and may everything come right for you.

Your loving Mums.

'Nervy' she may from time to time have been, but Zem stayed loving, businesslike and practical to the end.

And my mother took her advice very much to heart. She treated Aunt Flo as a mother and confidante for the rest of her aunt's life.

Aunt Flo is, of course, the Good Aunt of this book's title. I, sadly, never met her, but I owe her a debt of gratitude, not least for keeping my mother's letters from Africa.

With great indignation, Cissie was sent back to school. " I am so sorry you are lonely, I want to be with you", she wrote to her father. "At school," said Nancy Gee, "she wept for nearly the whole term. We did feel sorry for her, but…"

Life had to go on. Doctor Powell continued in practice, single handed. Cissie helped him with his accounts, learning how the wealthier patients unwittingly subsidized the poorer ones on 'the panel'.

The war ended.

"At about twelve o'clock we heard cheers and church bells, and we all threw the lesson books in all directions and flew round yelling," wrote Cissie to her father from St. Leonards. "Then we got flags and hung them out of all the windows. Later we went down to the front where everyone was absolutely mad. Processions of soldiers with girls, and army wagons with officers and men on, caps back to front and a lot of them drunk. It was so exciting…"

Dr. Powell liked young people, and encouraged his children to bring home friends to stay, and to hold children's and charade parties, or 'tea dances'. Christopher was now a cadet at the Royal Naval College, Dartmouth, and occasionally brought back naval friends for the dances. This made the dances a success, as young men were in short supply, so many having died during the war.

Doctor Powell continued to hunt with the Whaddon Chase. Coming home late one day, his horse slipped and rolled on him when he was thrown off. His back was injured, complications set in, and he died from these.

All Stony Stratford and the village of Calverton went to his funeral, or lined the route to Calverton church, and the Wolverton Express published a full page obituary, together with letters of sorrow at his passing, and an appreciation of his work during his twenty three years as a doctor in the area.

So Cissie found herself an orphan, with a brother seven younger than herself to look after. She was not yet 21.

Chapter 4 – Early pioneering life

In January, 1921 my grandmother Gertrude Greenhow wrote a letter to her Bank Manager:-

"Dear Sir,

My son, Lieutenant M.W. Greenhow, hopes to go to Rhodesia in a few months, and he has to show the British South Africa Company that he can, when required, put down £2,500. I intend to give him this. If the Company refer to you as to my financial position I should be much obliged if you could satisfy them.

I am yours faithfully,

G.M.P. Greenhow."

The die was cast. By April my father had his letter of credit from Cox and Co., and had cleared up everything. By May he was staying with an old school friend on that friend's farm in Rhodesia, whence he wrote to his mother:

"I walked about 18 miles yesterday to see a farm which they offer ex-servicemen at half price. It is certainly lower priced than anything I could get here, but is an awfully bad farm and would never be worth anything however hard I worked. I don't think I should ever be able to sell it as it is partly bad soil fit only for cattle, and the rest is all rock...

I have been all over the farm next to this one which is on a different estate and very expensive. However, I can see for myself it is good - it is all in one big valley, is only 2000 acres and the price asked is about a pound an acre. The more I look at it the more I like it, but the price is very stiff..."

After much soul searching and worrying about his mother's finances, he made up his mind, and on 1st September signed a Memorandum of Agreement to purchase 537 morgen (or 1,137 .78 acres) of land known as, " part of the Lawrencedale Estate in the Makoni district of Manica land". The vendors reserved all mineral rights, and the price was £1,706 =13s=5d.

Although then remote, my father chose a well situated farm. Its Western boundary lay right alongside the railway line which ran from Beira in Portuguese East Africa all the way to Umtali in Southern Rhodesia and thence to Salisbury, the capital. It was roughly halfway between Salisbury and Umtali, which were about 180 miles apart. A railway halt - Baddeley Siding - was only 2 miles away. In addition, the main road from Salisbury to Umtali ran along the farm boundary, which lay between the railway and the farm. This road was then an un-surfaced dirt road, which often became impassable in the wet season.

On the Northern boundary stood an immense kopjie, brooding over the farm and dominating the surrounding countryside. It was called Ruanda. Harry Lay had taken its name for his farm, so my father called his `Chigwani', the African name for a smaller kopjie on his land. On top of Ruanda kopjie was a beacon marking the surrounding farm boundaries. This beacon stood 5,521 feet above sea level, and 400 feet above its surroundings.

A valley with a small stream ran through the middle of the farm and under the skirts of Ruanda. In the low areas there were wet areas known as vleis, a South

African word, as is 'kopjie'. Here grew long grass and reeds in which Red and Yellow Bishop Birds, and Black Widow Birds with their long floppy tails bobbed up and down and nested in spring. During the wet season wild Red Hot Poker plants flared their red and yellow flowers there too. The best soil was red, similar to that in Devon, and lay close to Ruanda. The maize grown on this soil was conveniently placed for the baboons which lived on the kopjie to steal. They could retreat back into their stronghold at the first sign of danger.

Being so high above sea level the air was thin, which had an enervating effect on those not acclimatized to it. It was cooler at this altitude than in the lower parts of the country and there were fewer mosquitoes, which meant that malaria was not a problem. The Eastern Highlands of Inyanga, a very beautiful part of the country, were not far off and were visible on a clear day. In winter frosts occurred together with cold grey days, when a thin mist known as a 'guti' drifted over the countryside. Rain fell between late October and March in a good year, when an inch of rain in an hour was common place, and you could not hear a word but HAD TO SHOUT due to the roar of the downfall on the corrugated iron roof.

The years from 1921 to 1924 were hard. My father lived in three native style huts (living room, bedroom and kitchen) with thatched roofs under the lee of the big kopjie close to the stream which provided water.

First accommodation for Maurice on his new farm

He never had then, and indeed we never had later, such
amenities as piped water, electricity, modern sanitation
or telephones, which are now regarded as necessities.
Loneliness must have been the worst thing with which
he had to live. The bible truly says, "it is not good that
the man should be alone." It was three years before he
acquired a car, and there were few neighbours. In the
wet season the local roads and even the main Salisbury
to Umtali road could be impassable. Passenger trains
were limited to three each week, and the train journey to
Salisbury took over three hours due to the frequent halts.
I do not recall him telling of any Africans living on his land
other than those he employed, although the kopjies bore
past signs of habitation.

Letters to his mother tell of two drought years,
followed by a year of floods, and of constant financial
fears. The high initial cost of the land had left him with

insufficient money for other farming necessities. The land had to be cleared before it could be cultivated, fencing needed to be erected to keep cattle, and machinery, seeds and livestock needed to be purchased. Crops and cattle required time to grow and mature before they could be sold; meanwhile wages and living expenses had to be paid. All the while he was loath to ask for more funds from his mother, although he had not yet received all she had promised.

A small legacy of £300 kept him going for a while, but he eventually wrote:-

"I still need to build and furnish a house, and to have a cattle dip, more fencing, a hay mower and a store for tools. They cannot be called luxuries..."

In August, 1923 Gertrude wrote to her solicitor:-

"... I am thinking of going to Maurice in April. If I can get better for the journey the change might be quite good for me. I think I shall want about £200 to go, then I shall need to help Maurice - say about £350. He has always been a good son. We don't fill this house without him..."

Chapter 5. My mother's life with her young brother.

Life was difficult for my mother after her father died in 1922. Following the death of her mother in 1917 a governess had been found for Cissie's youngest brother Sam, who was only eight. Miss Boggis, or 'Bug', as she became known, was devoted to Sam, and Bug it was who took over the running of Calverton House. On leaving school Cissie was sent to Malvern Domestic College to learn such domestic skills as laundry work, cooking, dressmaking and housework. Housework lessons mainly consisted in scrubbing the floors of the college; cookery classes were limited to such basics as porridge, semolina, milk puddings and rissoles as a result of the food rationing. She returned home determined to demonstrate her domestic skills only to find, she said, that she hadn't any, and that Bug did everything better. This naturally led to tension between them. Meanwhile her brother Christopher was now a midshipman aboard the battle- cruiser H.M.S. Hood, recently commissioned and the pride of the Royal Navy, which was making a world cruise to 'show the Flag.' When he returned on leave my mother found him, "rather haughty and difficult".

Two trustees had been appointed to look after Sam's financial affairs; one was Aunt Flo, the other was an older sister of Doctor Powell. Aunt Emily had been born in 1856 and was a spinster with rigid Victorian views. She behaved as if my mother was intent on defrauding Sam of his rightful inheritance, demanding accounts for everything, and sending her letters asking:-

" Why Two tubes of toothpaste in One term?" or "Why So Many Cinema Tickets?"

The two trustees were an ill-assorted pair, and disliked each other. Cissie eventually resorted to applying to Aunt Flo for anything which she though needed prior approval, whereupon Aunt Emily complained that she was not being consulted. My mother developed a strong dislike of Victorian attitudes, and she afterwards confessed that she developed a dislike of old people for some time after this as well.

It was on Cissie's young shoulders that now fell the business of finding locums for the practise and then selling the practise together with Calverton House. Help arrived from an unexpected quarter. Dr. Powell had trained as a medical student at St. Thomas' Hospital and had made a friend there, who later became known as 'Uncle Nic'. Uncle Nic was no uncle, but a doctor who, after leaving St. Thomas', had had a rather chequered career. He had been through that unmentionable process, a divorce, and had also been made bankrupt. In the following hard times he had stayed at Calverton House with Dr. Powell until he found his feet again. He now proved a staunch friend. He it was who helped find locums, and he it was who, to her amazement and delight, took my mother to the Ritz for lunch on her twenty- first birthday, and followed this up by a visit to the theatre afterwards. In spite of the fact that Cissie had been chaperoned by Bug throughout this memorable day, Aunt Emily, who had done nothing to celebrate the occasion, thoroughly disapproved, and did not hesitate to say so afterwards

Locums lived in Calverton House while they were working for the practice, and one morning my mother was astonished to be casually handed a cheque for £2000 by one of them, a Dr. Hapgood, for his share of the practice. Dr Hapgood later bought Calverton House as well, where he brought up a son who later became an Arch Bishop of Canterbury.

After the house was sold, they stayed with Aunt Flo in Beaconsfield until a smaller house was found nearby, which they bought. Sam went to boarding school from whence, with much coaching, he graduated to a minor public school in Scotland. Sam inherited more than his fair share of the Peach family charm but he did not have his elder brother's scholastic ability, and he often failed exams. This was to be a constant worry for his elder sister.

For the next few years she looked after him during his school holidays. In summer they went to Exmoor, where a friend had started a riding school. There they discovered Badgery Water in the Doone valley, and stayed at Cloud Farm nearby with Mr. and Mrs. Locke thereafter. Mr. Locke was 'proper Devon', and often returned home on market days 'market 'mazed', as Mrs. Locke described his inebriated condition, which she accepted philosophically. She had several farm cats, to which she gave quantities of fish.

" Still hungry! Proper little ganders you be!" she would cry, refilling their plates.

Two of these cats were christened 'Mrs Popworthy' and 'Mrs Flesh-hanger' by the Powell guests. Mrs. Flesh-hanger was so named for her unpleasant habit of climbing up bare human legs using her claws. A verse was composed about these cats:-

"Mrs. Popworthy cat of Badgery Water

Got a lot more fish than she really oughter.

Poor Mrs. Fleshhanger went without it,

'Cos she didn't go the right way about it"

Other holidays were spent in France or in the Alps in winter. Because of a strong pound it was cheaper to take holidays abroad than in England.

Christopher was seldom at home now; he was often serving in Royal Naval ships abroad. Consequently he had little need for a house. Cissie started attending an Art School in London, so they sold the house in Beaconsfield, and she rented rooms in London. Here she made another friend for life in Miss Byrne, her landlady. When she returned to England after an absence of twenty - five years in Africa, as soon as she got to London she went to stay with Miss Byrne again.

Cicely Powell ('Cissie')

Cissie enjoyed her time at art school. She described the St. John's Wood School as rather old fashioned and run down. Life models sat in front of an old coke stove, and so were roasted red on one side, and frozen blue on the other. By tradition a 'celebrity' came at the end of each month to judge the pupils' compositions. Cissie remembered Alfred Munnings, Forbes Robertson and Ellen Terry coming, " all ancient and rather dilapidated, but magnificent none the less", she said. At St. John's Wood she learnt 'quick sketching from life', but later, realizing the limitations of what 'The Wood' had to offer, she went on to the more professional London School of Drawing. There she studied drawing from life, water-colouring, and wood cutting. She made many friends at the schools, and life with them and in London gave her a greater love and understanding of English Literature and poetry as well as Art.

The Great Strike took place. For this another of her verses remains for posterity:-
"An old gentleman said, " he'd like
To do some good work in the Strike"
So with manners most courtly
He offered each portly
Old lady a ride on his bike"
She did not take this historical event seriously, being uninterested in politics.

She made frequent visits to the theatre, including more than one to Nigel Playfair's production of 'The Beggar's Opera', which was very popular then. Her quick sketching skills were honed while she queued for theatre tickets, when she produced drawings, often coloured in water- colour later, of street acrobats, or a man with a tame blackbird which was trained to take a sixpence in its beak and drop it into a collecting tin. Street performers often provided entertainment for people in queues. It was a time when there was much unemployment...

One of the songs from the 'Beggars Opera' chimed with the times for Cissie and her friends:-
"Youth's the season made for joy..."
By 1928 Sam had left school, with an undistinguished

academic record, and no- one, least of all himself, quite knew what he was going to do for a living. But eventually he found an advertisement for an Agricultural School in South Africa, called the 1820 Settler's Training Farm. This was in the Eastern Cape, and he decided to enrol there to learn to farm. All too soon Cissie was seeing him on his way there aboard the Athlone Castle.

Chapter 6. My Grandmother's visit to Rhodesia in 1924.

On 10th April, 1924, Gertrude Greenhow sailed in the Dunluce Castle to visit Maurice in Rhodesia. She must have realized from the tone of his letters that he was having a hard time in his new life, so in spite of the fact that she had not been well, bravely she set forth, unaware of the discomforts she would face and all that would happen to her there. Her visit, planned eight months earlier, had spurred her son into action, and by the time she arrived a small brick farmhouse had been built, ready for her arrival. This house was situated on the boundary nearest to the main road which ran from Salisbury to Umtali,, beside which also ran the railway.

The bricks for this house were made on the farm, and were laid by my father to build the house. I remember seeing brick- making taking place when I was a child: the process was unchanged, so I will describe it.

What first drew me was the sound of Africans singing in the distance, and I hurried off to investigate. I found a large hole in the ground filled with wet clay in which a number of Africans were dancing up and down in their bare feet. This seemed a fascinating and very pleasant pastime on a hot sunny day to a five year old, and the Africans evidently thought so too, for they were singing as they worked, first one taking the lead, and then another, with the others working out rich harmonies. They were puddling the clay, to produce the malleable mix free from air suitable for the bricks. A hole some three or four feet deep had been dug beside the clay pit, and once the clay was ready the foreman jumped down into it. A wooden mould in the shape of three bricks was slid in front of him at waist height, and he threw lumps of clay into it to fill each corner. The remainder of the mould was then filled in, and he finished by striking off the surplus and levelling the top with a separate piece of wood. This was done with a great flourish for the benefit of the 'piccaninny baas'; it was also the signal for the mould to be removed by another worker, who upended it on a long level piece of sand nearby. The process was repeated until a line of wet bricks stretched away; these were covered with straw to dry out gently in the hot African sun. When dry they were built into a kiln and 'fired' with a wood fire until 'burnt'.

Brick Kiln and drying bricks on Chigwani

Gertrude kept a diary, and here is her description of the house when she arrived:-

"...a red brick bungalow built three rooms in a line, a living room between two bedrooms, and a kitchen behind the middle. The inside is pretty, the sitting room is pale blue with a wooden ceiling and a large corner fire with a double mantel shelf. The floor is cement and a large skin serves as a hearth rug. My bedroom is pale pink and has a mosquito proof blind in front of the window. Native made mats are on the floor..."

Maurice had obviously made it as attractive as he could for his mother. It had the inevitable corrugated iron roof so common in the colony, and was later to have a veranda added to the front. There was no bathroom, but from a small home- made dictionary I found at the back of her diary, two of the first words Gertrude learnt of the African dialect were "cheesa manzi", which meant 'hot water'. So there was probably a tin bath tub. Cement floors were necessary as white ants ate anything of wood at ground level.

Gertrude had arrived at Beira over a month after sailing from Tilbury. Maurice met her there and they took the train which steamed through Portuguese East Africa to Umtali on the Rhodesian border and then on towards Salisbury. They arrived at Baddeley Siding, the dusty unloved little halt about a mile from the farm, around midday on 19th May, 1924. Rhodesian trains had an open platform at the rear of each coach, from which three vertical steps descended to the platform below. My grandmother was tired by the long journey, she had ascended from sea level to an altitude of five thousand five hundred feet above that, and the strong sunlight dazzled her.

"I think I should be laboriously dismounting still," she wrote, "if Maurice had not lifted me bodily down". She was only 57, and she had not been well.

Harry Lay, Maurice's school friend from Lancing, together with Harry's mother were there to meet them. Gertrude's boxes were packed on a sleigh drawn by 12 oxen to be taken to Chigwani by Maurice's 'boys', as African servants were described then. My father had evidently still not been able to afford a wagon. A sleigh was made by felling a suitably forked tree; the V-shaped fork was trimmed to size and covered with planks, and the oxen were yoked to the butt end. On the way to the Lay's, Gertrude made some comment about the road, to be told by Mr. Lay that it was one of the best farm roads in the country. She made a mental note that, if this was true, she had a great deal of sympathy for all the other farmer's wives in Rhodesia.

She had lunch and a rest at the Lays, while Maurice walked the three miles back to Chigwani to collect his car. This was, "an ancient open- topped Ford, which had seen better days, but went all right".

Her first impressions of the countryside around, after descending from the train and being driven to Chigwani, were:-

"I saw a wide stretching sandy coloured plain with a few trees and many very curious rocks growing out of it in a detached sort of way. I later realised these rocks look different colours at different times of the day. They are most interesting; they look as if giants had been at play and dropped them all hap hazard. Lone kop is a beautiful one. In many kopjies it looks as if this or that stone must topple over: one looks like Humpty Dumpty, another like a squatting frog. In another I always see a black face in the mornings; in the afternoon it is gone. Burnt colour grasses, bushes and trees grow on the bigger outcrops and baboons live among them…"

Kopjies were always the most exciting places for my brother and I, and we spent a great deal of our holidays exploring and climbing them.

Early photographs support her description of there being few trees then. My memory, much later, is of there being a great many. They increased rapidly as a result of my father taking measures to prevent veldt - fires by creating fire breaks, and controlling grazing by cattle. These were confined in fenced paddocks, a practice never observed by Africans, who let theirs wander at will, tended by a piccannin. He also planted avenues and plantations of eucalyptus and other species, which transformed the landscape over the years.

Gertrude stayed with him for eight long months. She must have found it lonely, but she never complained. During the winter months the diet on the farm was Spartan; she missed fresh fruit. The orchard with orange, tangerine, grapefruit, plum and pawpaw trees that I remember had not yet been planted. Scots neighbours some distance away lived almost entirely on boiled eggs, which were always boiled since they did not have a frying pan. They were very stupid she thought. Beef could be purchased at sixpence a pound; if they sold a few dozen eggs they could have bought some beef.

I still have some of the letters which she wrote home. Here are some extracts:-

"I watched Maurice laying bricks this morning, quite fascinating. It is back-breaking work until you reach waist height. I am glad there are no Unions here. He once laid before breakfast the maximum number which a bricklayer is allowed to lay in a day in England - three hundred!"

Maurice, brick laying.

"Some people came today who, three months ago, brought us some tangerines which were most acceptable. Today they brought a few peas and some new potatoes. They have a garden and plenty of water. I hope to sample more of their fruit later on. Maurice thinks that you can buy a basket of mixed fruits around Christmas. That will be a great boon.

At present we have no butter and very little milk. Not enough to make even a milk pudding, so catering is difficult. The ordinary and not rich Rhodesian only eats what he can produce on his farm. I am glad to say Maurice buys both bread and meat in deference to me..."

Gertrude, from her comment about milk puddings, was obviously trying to produce proper meals for her son.

After two years of drought the wet season arrived with a vengeance that year. She kept a record of the weather conditions, noting thunder lightening and rain all together on thirty out of thirty five days in November and December, together with over ten inches of rainfall. At the back of her diary she also wrote a list of implements and equipment still needed on the farm. These included:- Wagon, Maize Sheller, Maize Planter, Disc Harrow, Mowing Machine, Large Plough, Cultivator, Fencing.

She had not yet given Maurice all the money she had promised, and he was loath to ask for it, since he knew it would reduce her income. By January she was once again feeling unwell, and she had to return to Salisbury to lodgings where she could rest and be cared for.

But by then she had been able to see the difficulties with which her son was coping herself, and before she left she arranged for a new fence to be erected along the boundary of the farm adjoining the main road.

Once she was in Salisbury, and feeling a little better, she started to plan her return home. In a letter to her daughter she wrote:-

"I shall look out for a letter from you at Cape Town, where we shall be from about 2nd to 9th June. Mail Boats take 18 days out from London and leave on a Friday, so you can calculate dates of posting, address - Post Office,

Cape Town. And, of course, wire me if you have anything to tell me or business to transmit. I could send you a wireless from the ship; they are not very dear.

See dictionary for words Boarder and Border. Do you really wish me to keep the former for the gardener to amuse? I am rather glad you have a new gardener for me – the other arrangement was not very good.

Yesterday the water supply here gave out, and the proprietor asked me if I would mind using "a little apartment" at the old house a few yards away. I hunted about the old house and found none. But I did find a cow (as I thought) lying down in a room with the door shut. It turned out to be a missing ox, which disappeared two days ago, but the fool of a herd boy never told anyone! Mr Olave, who looks after the estate, says he has never heard of an ox walking into a dining room and shutting the door behind it before! He has now got buckets of water being carried up for us, and a new pipe is being put on the hydraulic ram..."

She then decided to see the Victoria Falls before she left the country. But once there she suffered a heart attack, and died. Her gravestone read;-

In Memory of Gertrude Mary Petch Greenhow
Who fell asleep on 25th April, 1925.

Chapter 7. My mother goes to Africa. My parents' wedding

After Sam had sailed for South Africa, my mother courageously decided she must follow him to keep an eye on him. She also discovered that there was an Agricultural College for women called Boschetto near Harrismith in South Africa. She had better learn something about farming, she thought, so she could be in a better position to help to him, so she arranged a meeting with the principal of that college, who was in London at that time. The principal, a forthright woman, said that Cissie, "looked the ideal sort", a rather left-handed compliment Cissie thought. The principal also told her that Third Class on the Arundel Castle would be perfectly acceptable. It was in fact crowded and uncomfortable. My mother could, to use a Royal Naval phrase, feel seasick on a wet lawn, so was prostrated on the bunk of her stuffy shared cabin until the ship reached the Azores, where the sea became calmer.

While recovering she met a quiet sympathetic man called Maurice. He was returning to Rhodesia after visiting England, whence he had had to return to deal with legal problems arising from his mother's will. I do not think that they could have conversed a great deal, since he was travelling second class and she was in third.

But they did recognize each other at a chance meeting nearly a year later.

Boschetto Agricultural College had fairly primitive domestic facilities by English standards. The students also did most of the manual work on the College farm, and there were not a great many students for this work, so they were kept busy. Nevertheless it had a jolly atmosphere. The sanitation arrangements were colonial, with earth closets for the girls, and my mother was asked by the principal to put a notice in these instructing all those students who were used to water closets how earth closets should be used. Nothing daunted, she composed this little rhyme:-

"I'm sorry to trouble, you see,
But this is not a W. C.
So in view of the queue
That comes after you
Put in ash with the shovel.
Merci!"

At Boschetto my mother learnt and practiced such skills as butter making, poultry plucking, dairy work, calf feeding, double digging and bee keeping. The latter skill was never followed up, as during her practical examination, she was asked to find the Queen Bee. While she was searching for it another bee worked its way up her britches and stung her, whereat she dropped the frame with an oath. She failed the exam, and received a mild reproof from the Zulu foreman,

" Inkosikaas, we no swear here!"

She felt far worse for the reproof than when she heard she had failed, she said.

At the end of two terms at the college she met up again with Sam. His agricultural school had not been a success; all he had learnt was that he was not cut out to be a farmer. He thought he would try to be a vet instead. My poor mother was at a loss. All her brave efforts to encourage and help him had come to nothing. Neither did she think (rightly as it turned out) that he would be successful in passing the entrance exams for veterinary college. She decided to go to Southern Rhodesia where an old friend, Daphne King, had invited her to stay before returning to England via the East coast of Africa.

Daphne was living with her father in Salisbury, where her father Godfrey King was working as an administrator appointed by Cecil Rhodes in the capital. Cissie decided that, with his walrus moustache, he looked rather like the White Knight in 'Alice in Wonderland.' The Kings lived in a typical colonial house, complete with corrugated iron roof and wide verandah, in Borrowdale on the outskirts of the city. Mr. King bicycled to work, except during the rains. He changed into a dinner jacket and black tie every evening for dinner, which the family ate on the verandah by the light of guttering candles which attracted many moths. The kitchen was detached from the house, so the food was usually tepid by the time it arrived. Daphne sported an Eaton Crop hair style, and did not much care for fashion or housework, which did not prevent her from having numbers of admirers, Cissie noticed.

One of Mr. King's duties was the registration of all motorcars in Rhodesia. Since the number of white people in Rhodesia was then about 30,000 (less than the population of Eastbourne) and cars were rare, this part of his work was not onerous, but nonetheless he had dutifully registered his own car when he bought it, and allocated the unique number plate 'S 1' to himself when so doing, thereby upstaging the governor of the colony.

The Kings were very kind and hospitable and when the time came, insisted that Cissie went with them to the major social event of the colony, the ball after the annual Salisbury Agricultural Show. This Show was attended by every farmer in the country who was able to put one leg in front of the other. Hotel accommodation in town was impossible to obtain while it went on, unless it had been booked months before hand. At this ball whom should my mother meet but the quiet, good looking gentleman who had been so sympathetic to her on board the 'Arundle Castle', Maurice Greenhow. Although he was never one who liked big social events, he must have felt the need to see a bit of civilisation, and to get away from the farm, as so many others on remote farms also did. The opportunity to keep up to date with agricultural innovations at the Agricultural show also provided a conscience saving excuse: in any event it turned out to be a life changing moment for both him and my mother.

After the Ball the Kings invited Maurice to lunch the following day, and thereafter he kept in touch. Indeed he made so many journeys from the farm to Salisbury and back in his old Ford car that, one by one, its tyres gave out and burst. Maurice and Cissie soon became "very fond of each other", and in due course they were married in Salisbury Cathedral on 12th November, 1930. My mother was driven to her wedding in car registration number S 1 by Godfrey King, who then 'gave her away'. Had she known that she would not return to England for another twenty five years she might have made one last visit 'home' before the wedding she said later.

Chapter 8. The new Farmhouse. My brother's Birth

After their wedding my parents went to the Victoria falls for their honeymoon, then it was back to the farm. It was their last holiday away together for twelve years.

It had taken several years for my Grandmother Gertrude's will to be settled. The terms were simple; her estate was to be divided equally between her two remaining children, my father and his sister. But his sister contested it, saying that my father had been lent the money to buy his farm, not given it, and that this money should therefore be repaid into their mother's estate. My father disagreed. His mother's letter to her bank manager had specifically said, " I intend to give him this..." He was therefore not only quite sure that his mother had given him the money, but also knew that his sister had had her share of their mother's money before her death. A sad family squabble was the consequence. The old family solicitor was little help, since his letters seemed to take a very long time being composed in his Dorset office, and an even longer time in arriving at Baddeley siding in Southern Rhodesia, where the mail was dropped off the train once a week in a canvas bag. This was why Maurice had been forced to return to England to settle matters.

But he inherited some money at last and with a

new wife to support, this was rapidly spent on a new farmhouse and other improvements to the farm. A description of the new house was given in a letter from Cicely to her cousin:-

"Our new home is jolly fine. It's still not finished, 'tho we've been in it now three months. The sitting and spare rooms have no doors or ceilings yet, nor distemper. Ceilings are a problem - plaster ones aren't used out here. So it's either steel (otherwise tin) with hideous embossed patterns, or boards, or calico. We have a steel one of the plainest possible kind in the dining room. Maurice whitewashed it, and it has gone rusty already! Our bedroom has one of canvas, and looked very nice until a rat made nasty little stains and gnawed a hole.

"Floors are of cement, because of ants. Painful but necessary and, when coloured red and polished like ours, they are like skating rinks.

"The whole house cost under £300, including making and hauling bricks. It has a large verandah on three sides, five rooms and pantry, kitchen and bath. Maurice built it mostly himself. We also now have a windmill for the well. We borrowed from the land bank to do both."

The farmhouse nearing completion (my father on the roof)

Foundations for the house had been completed in January 1931 shortly after my mother arrived. During the rest of that year there was much other activity. A well was excavated near it, which needed blasting with dynamite to remove rock. Over it a windmill was erected which pumped water up to a corrugated iron tank on metal legs behind the new house. The overflow from this tank fell into a stone-built reservoir beneath, to provide water for vegetables and fruit trees, and which was intended to supply piped water to the house. Alas it never did; water was thereafter always carried in buckets to the house. The buckets were made from old two gallon paraffin tins, with a wooden handle made from a branch nailed inside the top. Carrying the cans was part of the house-boy's 'sebenze' (work).

A new mower and hay rake were purchased. The

livestock was increased, with a new bull and some more poultry. Fruit trees were planted to make an orchard. By July the house was ready for a carpenter to come and put up the timber frames for the corrugated iron roof.

The requirement for a larger house became apparent on 27th September, 1931 when my brother Kenneth was born. He arrived in state in the Lady Chancellor Nursing home in Salisbury. On my mother's return she was able to spend her first night in the new house, now habitable but not quite completed.

A new hot water system was built later, to be welcomed amongst Cissie's all too infrequent diary entries, "Hot Bath!"

The system was common on Rhodesian farms; I remember its like in other places. A recycled forty five gallon petrol drum was built into an outdoor brick furnace, with a space under the drum for a log fire and a chimney at the closed end. A pipe from the bottom of the drum led direct into the bathroom adjoining. It was the houseboy's job each evening to fill the drum with water and to light and attend to the wood fire beneath it. The system, alas, had all too short a life. Africans became sleepy once the sun went down, which it unfailingly did at about half past six. (Long summer evenings extending to ten o'clock were unknown to me until I came to England). The task of filling the drum by hand with buckets of water which had to be carried some fifty yards was not a popular one either. One chilly evening the house boy lit a cheery blaze in the furnace to warm himself, having 'forgotten' to fill the drum beforehand. The fire melted the bottom of the drum which had no water in it to keep it at a water boiling temperature. The houseboy, when he woke up to find this, immediately went to the 'missus' to ask for a day off, as his sister was ill. Quite who had brought him this tragic news at such convenient short notice remained a mystery, but he departed before the 'boss' arrived back for his bath, and was not seen until a week later, by which time he hoped the matter had been forgotten. It had not, and ever after the houseboy, whoever he was, was required to heat our bathwater in two old paraffin tins placed over an outdoor fire and to carry the tins to fill our bath. The brick furnace had been built so well that it would have been a major undertaking to remove the damaged drum and replace it. The outdoor system meant that if it was raining the water had to be heated over the old Dover cast iron stove in the kitchen. This took forever, so baths were usually tepid on these occasions

Paraffin was used for lamp oil, there being no electricity supplies except in the main cities. It came in rectangular tins holding two gallons, which were packed in pairs in sturdy wooden boxes. Both tins and boxes were recycled once the paraffin had been used. The tins, with a round piece of timber from a branch cut to fit and nailed to the inside rim to form a handle, made useful water containers, which could also be heated over a fire. The boxes were converted into all sorts of furniture. I can remember them as bedside tables with curtains in front concealing an internal shelf. They could also be made into a meat safe by cutting the panels to form a framework, fitting a door frame and door, and covering the frame with wire gauze. We had one suspended on a wire from a ceiling joist in our larder. I made myself useful by shooting with my air gun a rat which had come down the wire once.

By 1932 the World Depression had set in, and the

country was severely affected. Prices for farm products fell well below those received in 1920 and farmers struggled to make ends meet. Scots neighbours had a mortgage which was 'called in', but were allowed to stay on as caretakers. When war came later, by hard work and by starting a dairy and by growing tobacco, they were able to buy back the farm and became quite prosperous. Other neighbours fell into a state of apathy or lived on the generosity of relatives. One borrowed money from Maurice to buy a bull. The money was never repaid. My father would not press the matter, but neighbourly relations never recovered.

Social life suffered; there was little money for entertaining, or the petrol required to visit. However, there were interesting callers occasionally. One was a 'wallaby' as he called himself. A more accurate description was that he was an Australian tramp. Maurice regarded him as a gentleman tramp, who rationed his visits and never outstayed his welcome. On his previous call Maurice had been a bachelor; finding a new bride in the house he refused to come in. He was persuaded to sleep on the verandah, and went away after a good breakfast the next day, never to return.

Other callers were a couple who were touring the country with a view to settling for health reasons. They arrived at the unfinished back of the house, and were retreating hastily when discovered. Once installed on the front verandah, which was by then completed, and given tea, they had little hesitation in accepting beds for the night. Fresh faces, any English faces, were always welcome.

In July, 1932 truly welcome guests arrived. Sam, Cicely's younger brother, being still at a loose end, had announced his intention in advance, but who should he find on the Arundle Castle which brought him out but Cissie's old school friend, Nancy Gee. Nancy indignantly denied that she had either followed or enticed him out, but she may have saved his life on the way. Sam, like Cissie, had a very light head as far as alcohol was concerned, and after a shipboard cocktail party Nancy went on deck to get some fresh air and found Sam blithely walking along the ship's rail on his hands, watching the waves go by underneath him. She quickly grabbed his belt and hauled him back inboard.

They both provided help and much- needed company for my parents. Maurice was delighted, as there was now a foursome for bridge in the evenings. He had acquired a liking for card games in the prisoner of war camp. Nancy helped look after Kenneth, and the chickens. Sam set to shelling the maize crop, and when that was completed he proceeded to level and lay a tennis court. The surface of this was finished with earth dug out of large termite mounds which were common on the farm. The termite saliva in this earth caused it, when dampened and rolled, to make a good hard surface. Once completed, the possession of a tennis court meant that neighbours could be invited to play, and return invitations followed. Maurice was good at the game and Cissie a staunch player who amazed opponents with an underarm service, which proved not as easy to return as it looked as it had disconcerting dip and spin. Young Kenneth always accompanied them to tennis parties. At one farm eighteen miles away there was a grandmother who thanked Cissie with tears in her eyes for bringing a baby, because it was so long since she had seen a white baby, she said. This old lady insisted on coming to Chigwani for the next tennis party, and wedged herself in between her son and his wife in their two-seater car to do so. Cissie thought this very sporting.

Sam decided to do some prospecting, and gold fever descended on the farm. Slight traces were found, but then Maurice sadly remembered that mineral rights were not included with his land, and the prospecting came to an end.

Sam then decided to explore the big kopjie. Africans seldom went near it. I never found on it the traps and snares which they laid for game and birds everywhere else. It was reputed to be 'tagati', which meant it was a forbidden place associated with witch doctors. On it, they said, was a cave in which there was a big drum, and anyone beating on this drum would die. There was no stopping Sam once he had heard about this, and he and Maurice together eventually found both cave and drum. The drum was brought back, together with a human skull from this cave and both were photographed on the verandah of the old house. Cissie always said that these should never have been touched, and that they had brought bad luck.

The drum with the curse from Ruanda Kopjie

Years later I found the same cave. It was hidden three quarters of the way up the kopjie, in the steepest and most inaccessible part of it. It was large and dark and eerie and in it I found the remains of a second drum, which was not in such good condition as the first. I left it well alone, and backed out quickly, feeling rather frightened. African superstitions can be catching.

Contrasting letters were sent back to Aunt Flo during this time. Nancy reported that:-

"Kenneth is a perfect pet, and a great credit to his mother. Cissie, on the other hand, looks run down and nervy, probably due to too much work and worry after K. was born."

My mother, however, wrote with glee,

" Nancy has got fatter, while I have got thinner, so we both now weigh the same, about ten stone."

My mother always regretted that she had not inherited

the willowy grace of her mother, instead of the strong frame of the Powell side of her family. But with all the farm work she had recently taken on, (she was looking after calves, chickens, the vegetable garden and the dairy work as well as a young baby), there was good reason for her to have lost weight. With Nancy there to look after my brother, Sam was able to take Cissie to Salisbury to buy furniture, collect her beloved books and some of her other family possessions which had been shipped out, visit the dentist and see a 'talkie'. Another visit was made to christen Kenneth just one day before he reached his first birthday, Sam and Nancy being conveniently to hand for god parents.

Nancy loyally stayed on helping for several months, but Sam became restless, and departed for England via Kenya, where he had an invitation. It was a visit which changed the whole focus of his life; exploring some of the remoter areas, including Lamu, he became entranced by the exotic and wilder parts, and he spent the rest of his short life exploring all over central and Northern Africa, seldom returning to England for long.

So, when Nancy left near the end of the year, my parents were alone again.

Chap. 9. An English child in an African World

After Nancy's departure, Africa began to show its hard implacable nature. In England there remains a view that farming is a 'way of life', and that a life in the countryside is idyllic. And England is, away from its dark satanic mills, a green and pleasant land with few dangers in its country side more dangerous than wasps or nettles. But Africa, although it possesses an attraction all its own, particularly for men, also has a climate of extremes, wildlife that is dangerous, destructive or both, and pests and diseases that are deadly to both man and his livestock.

In 1932 there was yet another drought. This was followed the following year by heavy rains, and, just as the new crops were breaking into delighted green life, swarms of locusts descended to eat everything in their path. One swarm in the country was reported as being fifteen miles long and three miles wide and many farmers lost everything.

During this time Cissie took her baby in his pram for a walk in the veldt, accompanied by her beloved dogs. They found and attacked a cobra in the long grass. She hurried away, calling the dogs after her. During lunch that day two of them died under the table from the venom from the snake's bites.

Maurice caught 'tick fever', a tropical disease transmitted by the bite of a tick. This put him in hospital for a fortnight, and left him weak for several months afterwards.

Meanwhile the World Financial Depression continued, with the result that prices for agricultural produce continued to fall. But life had to go on.

Daphne King, the friend who had originally invited my mother to Southern Rhodesia, had married an Irishman who farmed at a place called Wedza. After the birth of their daughter June, my mother was invited to stay. For the last part of her journey there Cissie sat on mealie sacks with Kenneth on her lap in the back of their farm lorry as it jolted over the dusty corrugated road. The journey took three hours to cover forty five miles. As a result Kenneth's eyes swelled up and became inflamed. In a panic, " fearing some dreadful African complaint", my mother took him to a doctor, who diagnosed conjunctivitis, and made some scornful remark about "these mothers with only children" which touched her on the raw. The visit did, however, produce a hint of her old humour with this dreadful composition, which must have been in answer to a challenge to find a rhyme for 'Wedza'.

"There once was a farmer of Wedza,
Whose manager came and said, " Sir,
I don't wish to alarm,
Or raise the whole farm.
But there's a python asleep on your bed, Sir!"

Daphne Searson, as she now was, consulted my mother about baby care. "A fat lot I know about babies," my mother said afterwards. But she did not give herself enough credit, for she indomitably continued to rear my brother throughout these troubled years in the way she thought best. He learnt good manners, and she read him Beatrix Potter; what better things should a child learn in a remote corner of Africa? Beatrix Potter readings became something he could not do without during his supper, to the extent that once, when neighbours came to call and interrupted this ritual, he was heard to say, "I do wish these damn Kellies would go away". The books were demanded over and over again until he knew them by heart. During one supper his well laden spoon paused halfway on its journey. " Why aren't you eating?" he was asked. "I'm going to laugh at the next bit," he replied, "so I'm not filling my mouth yet until it's over". Magazine pictures of the Silver Jubilee were viewed by him with great interest. One of the king without a crown received the comment " he's not wearing his crown, he must be indoors."

An English boy in an African setting.

The fact that a small child in a remote part of the colonies should know that a hat, even if it is a crown worn by his King, must only be worn out of doors, shows the emphasis put on his learning good manners by his parents.

In 1935, probably in response to one of Cissie's many letters saying how much she missed England, the family received an invitation from Aunt Flo to return to England for a holiday and to stay with her. This provoked a major difference of opinions, and my parents' replies make sad reading:

"I have had a great struggle not to book a passage." wrote Cissie. " I got as far as enquiring about sailings, but my heart failed me. M. does seem to hate the idea so... If you knew how homesick I get these days..."

An all too rare letter from my father when replying to this invitation gives an insight into his thoughts on the subject:-

"I must apologise for not answering sooner. There is no chance of writing in the day due to the hopeless unreliability of the native, and the endless jobs which are waiting to 'get done' in between times. Between 7.30 p.m and 9 p.m. (we go to bed later than many) after the farm business has been dealt with, one gets an hour to read or relax in, and the arm chair usually wins.

With prices at or below the cost of production one doesn't know which way to turn now...Tradesmen are extraordinarily good in not worrying unduly for settlement, and it is well known that they have been 'carrying' much of the farming community. The Land Bank has fifty-three farms on its hands, bought - in at auction when the owners sold up. But the commercial fraternity do not foreclose, as they know that they would only get 2s/- in the £, and the farmer has a reputation for settling in full in the long term. So it is not an opportune time for taking expensive holidays..."

My father's conviction that work must come first, and his belief that he must not incur any more debts, are clear. A return to England for the whole family would undoubtedly have been expensive. There was also the question as to who would have supervised the farm in his absence. Farm work never stops as animals have to be milked, herded and fed, and once a crop is harvested preparations have to be made for the next, or a year goes by with no income. One uncontrolled veldt fire in his absence would have undone years of hard work, and the Africans certainly could not have been trusted to prevent one. Indeed they often started them when smoking out wild bees, or on some similar escapade. Nevertheless, a short break now and then would have been good for him and his wife.

An account of a row between my parents which took place at about this time was given by my mother years later. My mother became so angry during this that she picked up a missile to throw at him. The nearest to hand proved to be the unfortunate cat which was sitting on my mother's lap. It scratched his face when landing, but all my father said then was, "don't take it out on the cat". My mother blushed when she described this; when she did, it reminded me of my father's good manners.

The farm was still being improved. An avenue of Jacaranda trees was planted up the avenue leading to the front of the house, and Eucalyptus and pines round it which gave shade and shelter. Later, when I slept on the verandah, the soft sighs of the breeze breathing through the needles of the big pine outside remain a very happy memory.

A line of Cyprus trees screened the farm road in front, and mulberries lined one side of the tennis court. A much needed garage for the canvas roofed car was built. A bigger challenge was provided by the new cattle dip, in which the cattle had to be immersed once a week in the tick season to prevent tick- borne diseases. This building with its angles, slopes, and long back -draining area into which the dipping liquid dripped once the animals had been immersed was far more difficult to build than the farm house, my father said. A Dutchman with the name Cloppers came to do the final waterproof internal rendering; I am surprised that, with a name like that, he departed without a limerick all to himself.

A further year went by until, in September 1936, another letter to Aunt Flo gave a new reason why a visit to England could not take place:

"...now I've been and gone and done it. Apparently I am increasing the family about next April... so I fear that when you eventually harbour us, there will be not one, but two children. I suppose, although there is a big gap between them, it is better late than never. One is a mistake... and I do so want a daughter.

Cissie."

Reader, beware! The author has almost made his appearance! He may, like Tristram Shandy, have been slow in making his arrival, but if you wish to wait no longer do not forget when leaving the scene to take Laurence Sterne's advice and "close the door!"

Chapter 10. A Birth, a Coronation and another War.

"My dearest Auntie Flo,

Just a line to tell you of our No. 2 son. I did want a daughter, but don't mind at all now he's here. He is to be Philip.

We are going home this afternoon. I greatly prefer this little hospital to being away in Salisbury.

This babe arrived in a great hurry - we nearly didn't get here in time. I came in twice, and was told each time to wait another two to three weeks. The second time we came in, (fourteen miles on a bumpy road) was the morning of the event, and even then the doctor said it couldn't be and that I must have indigestion! So we went home again, and at three p.m. had to come hurtling back to arrive five minutes before it arrived. The doctor had by then gone to Umtali seventy miles away, but the matron was most efficient and all was well without him...

Cissie"

In such a way I arrived in the world on 17th April, 1937. The above letter, headed 'Rusape Hospital' and dated 29th April, 1937, gives an insight into changes that had occurred in the colony since my father arrived in 1921. There was now a pleasant little hospital in Rusape, the nearest small town containing police and railway stations, a church and a few stores which were owned mostly by Indians. The hospital obviously also had an efficient matron, if a less competent doctor, and my mother stayed in it for twelve days after an uncomplicated birth. But the road to Rusape, which was also the main road to Umtali and the port of Beira, was still not tarred. It was not until 1939 that two strips of tarmac were laid to take the wheels of motor vehicles. After that cars approaching each other had each to get off one strip to allow the other to pass, a process that was difficult and unpopular and occasionally fatal. But Rusape was now sufficiently civilised for my mother to prefer the hospital there than that in Salisbury. (There had been no alternative when my brother was born).

After my birth a young Dutch girl came to help my mother with her two children. My brother was now five, and had to begin his schooling His mother therefore had the additional burden of being responsible for this. Nursery schools were few and far over the country, so correspondence courses for children who could not attend one were provided by the government. These courses were supervised by their parents, and were based on those used in the 'outback' in Australia. My mother found them a useful guide, and concentrated Kenneth's efforts on her favourite subjects, reading, art and nature study. Arithmetic was not her strong subject, so it did not receive quite the same attention. The Dutch girl, who had helped to raise seven sisters and a baby brother and therefore had plenty of experience with babies, proved "a treasure", and stayed for six months. Kenneth's nature studies required him to keep a nature diary. In this he listed and drew birds, beetles, butterflies and plants that he saw during the seasons and painted them with water colours. His studies bore fruit; birds in particular became the great interest of his later life.

Another historic event took place in England shortly after my birth - the Coronation of George VI. To commemorate this, my loyal father climbed the big kopjie and planted a stand of eucalyptus trees on the top. In 1989, when I revisited the farm after thirty five years absence, these trees still stood out proud and regal on the horizon, and could be seen from far away.

With two young children to look after, my mother settled down to make the best of things. The car was now showing signs of decrepitude. A trip to Salisbury had to be cancelled when it was discovered that the radiator could no longer hold water.

"It had to be torn off and sent away to be welded. Doubtless when it comes back it will un-weld itself, because the road is so full of corrugations," reported Cissie. The car was an open- topped model with a canvas hood, and side screens instead of windows. This meant that insects could easily penetrate inside, and the last straw came when a swarm of wild bees took possession one day. They proved difficult and painful to evict. On her next visit to the capital my mother exchanged it for a less decrepit saloon, without telling my father beforehand. She could be very stubborn sometimes.

I was now reaching the age where I could produce alarms of my own. One morning, when my mother was preparing for Christmas, she suddenly found the house unnaturally quiet. I had by this time become quite mobile, and instinct prompted her to look out of the back door. Some fifty yards away stood the stone reservoir which held water for the vegetable garden, seven feet deep, twelve feet wide, and with its rim five feet above ground level. On the edge she noticed two dogs looking intently into it. Up she rushed, and there I lay, on my back, my clothes like Ophelia's spread wide, as awhile they bore me up. After being fished out, and given a hot bath, I was none the worse, but my mother went hot and cold for a long time after whenever she thought about it.

Two cousins of my mother's, Hilda and Nancy Powell, who had shared 'the pink room' with her at school, came to stay in 1938. They had a good camera, and they left as a memento of their visit some excellent photographs. As well as family groups in front of the farmhouse, there were also panoric views of the farm, one from the top of the big kopjie. The "wide and featureless plain" described by my grandmother Gertrude when she arrived in 1925 was now unrecognisable. The photograph looking down on the farm shows a tree-shaded farmhouse in the distance, a seventy acre plantation of eucalyptus trees, one hundred and fifty acres of arable land, roads, avenues and a cattle dip. This photo now provides the front cover for this book.

But one year later in 1939 it was all to be abandoned for six years. There is a brief reference in a letter that my father wrote earlier that year that he was beginning to wonder whether he should give up farming. Hitler made the decision for him; when war was declared my father had no alternative in his own mind but that he had to serve his country. I cannot to this day imagine my father telling a lie, but when it came to joining up he was quite prepared to declare a birthday two years later than when it actually occurred, to make himself forty three rather than forty five, thus enabling him to re-enlist. He started life in the army as a 'ranker 'once again, this time sergeant Greenhow, in November 1939.

My mother was not prepared to stay on the farm all on her own with two young children to look after, so by that date all the livestock and machinery had been sold, the furniture moved out, and house and land were left to their own devices for the long weary years of the war.

Chapter 11. Early Memories.

Early morning, in April in Southern Rhodesia. The rains are over and gone and the voice of the turtle dove, the sound that for me distils Africa, can be heard in the lands.

"What is it saying" I asked.

" Some people say it says, 'Work harder! Work harder!' But others say it is calling, 'Where's father? Where's father?'

"Mummy, where is Daddy?"

"He's gone to the war."

The beginning of that lovely day began forebodingly. When I woke up there was a heavy weight pressing the blankets down on my feet. Could it be a leopard, waiting to pounce on me and eat me? I had heard a coughing noise in the kopjie while we were queuing for a bath at dusk the day before, and had been told it was a leopard. Then my fears dissolved; I knew what was at the bottom of the bed, and everything was wonderful after all.

It was not a leopard lying on my feet about to eat me, but Presents! Because it was my Birthday!

I was three.

The paper was torn off the largest parcel. "What's this?"

" It's a book. Let me see. From Aunt Flo. The story of Babar", replied my mother, dressing- gowned, and suppressing a yawn after being woken so horribly early.

"Ooh! Here's a green elephant. He looks very sick. Why's he green?"

" Oh dear! He's been poisoned. He ate something he shouldn't - bad mushrooms! Now get your shirt and shorts on, and I will read it all to you after lunch when I have my rest."

This is the earliest memory to which I can attach a date - 17th April, 1940. I was three.

April was in the autumn in Rhodesia. The wonderful flush of colour peculiar to the Rhodesian spring arrived six months later in October. This was near the end of the dry season, which was a period of six months when no rain fell. The end of this cruel time was heralded each year on the High Veldt by one of Nature's greatest displays, the flushing of the fresh leaves of the M'sasa trees. A glorious palette of reds, crimson and orange spread across the landscape wherever the Msasa and its cousins, the Mupfuti and the Mountain Acacia, flourished, promising a revival of growth all over the land once the rains had fallen. Nowhere else does it occur; Msasa trees do not grow south of the Limpopo river.

Chapter 12. Guard Duty and a School Fete

Christmas 1939 saw my father 'in camp' near Salisbury and my mother with her children staying on a farm near Marandelas. My father found himself, with a groan, sergeant of the guard on New Year's Eve. Being an old soldier, he knew that it was likely that there would be many soldiers overstaying their leave that night, so he turned back the hands of the guardroom clock just before midnight, by which time all leave was supposed to end. Early next morning, once the last drunk had just rolled in, he turned the clock back to show the correct time once more and was thus able to report, "All back before midnight by the guardroom clock, sir!" when a slightly hung over officer of the day appeared. The officer, if he suspected anything, sensibly refrained from comment. The careful phraseology of my father's report meant that no lie had been told.

My brother was now a boarder at a preparatory school near Marandelas called Ruzawi.

"We can ill-afford it, wrote my mother, but as Maurice is now on active service, we get a Government grant of £16 a term. Wives get £12-10s a month, which is very welcome, but poor Maurice makes do on 5s/- a day." In 1942 Maurice was sent to East Africa, where he received an emergency commission in August.

The owner of the farm where she was now staying was away on his honeymoon with his second wife. My mother was helping to look after the three children from his first marriage while he was away. A retired major was also there to look after the farm in the owner's absence, and had brought with him two children, four gundogs and a wife, so a noisy Christmas followed. The three children of the owner were extremely well brought up, which I apparently " found it hard to live up to." The farm had a big house, an excellent pedigree dairy herd and several race horses.

This luxurious existence came to an end all too soon, when the owner returned with his new wife. The major meanwhile had purchased a very beautiful farm near Marandellas, which was suitable for taking paying guests. This farm was only a mile from my brother's new school, and on it was a two bed- roomed cottage in which my mother forthwith became a paying guest, it being so convenient for her to see my brother at school at weekends.

Ruzawi School put on a Fete to raise funds to support the war effort. My mother had made friends with a young English Mistress at the school and was called upon to help. She produced dozens of posters advertising the Fete and the stalls. Meanwhile staff, parents and boys slaved away to produce things to sell on the great day. The older boys were put to making everything from bread boards to butter pats in the carpentry shop, while the younger ones made clay pots, wool mats, or hand sewn and knitted items. A disciplinary problem arose when a boy was found studying a knitting pattern book instead of one on history during 'prep'. I was never told whether he was punished or whether a discreet blind eye was turned to this awful sin.

When the day of the fete arrived, it started with an exhibition by the senior boys of P.T. using Indian Clubs. This was followed by a school play. Parents brought produce or other items for the stalls, and one brought donkeys to give donkey rides. Cissie made stuffed toys from materials which varied from old grey flannel shorts which came from the school to pink celanese which came from who knows where, and produced Eeyores, Piglets, Kangas (with baby Roos in their pockets), and Owls. All of these sold quickly as they were full of character, and toys were in short supply, since imports were restricted due to the war.

She took charge of Form Two's stall for an hour, so had to buy off it a bag with a string pull and a pine tree embroidered on it by my brother for an extortionate 1s/6d. During the hour my mother was in charge sales made at this stall raised over £37. This was three times the amount she was receiving in a month from my father's army marriage allowance! At the end of the day an auction was held to get rid of everything left unsold. The total amount raised by the fete was £720, an enormous sum then. Southern Rhodesians were very patriotic, and did everything they could to support Great Britain.

Rationing was now being enforced in England, so O.K. Bazaars in Salisbury were selling food parcels which could be sent 'home'.

"I am sorry they are rather mingy, but they have to be kept below a regulation size," said the letter accompanying one such parcel which Cissie sent to her aunt.

My father had by now been sent to Nairobi with the Rhodesian Transport Division, whence he expected to be posted to Abyssinia. His letters were infrequent, and took longer to reach my mother than those from England. My mother had to settle down for the duration but remained, "still determined to return home when this infernal war is over".

Chapter 13. Elephant Guns and Bathroom Queues

Major Fetlock had been wounded in the first world war, and like many other ex-servicemen, had decided to retire to Rhodesia, where the climate was warmer, there were fewer restrictions, and bigger things to shoot. He brought with him a big game rifle of awe- inspiring calibre, only to find that he was seldom able to use it, as all the big game in the area in which he chose to settle had long since either moved away to the hot dry lowland areas which were unhealthy for humans, or had been shot. I suspect that little serious farming was carried out on the farm he purchased, but the land it contained enabled him to keep a stable, and the house, cottage and buildings provided accommodation for paying guests, who could be lured thither by the promise of riding. The farmhouse was full of cartridge belts, shooting sticks, broken bits of saddlery and gun dogs eating smelly objects they had found in the veldt. The only books in the house were the Jorrocks books, by Surtees. Mrs Fetlock battled daily to keep her paying guests fed and happy, mollifying them with cups of tea when her husband upset them or was rude to them. There was only one bathroom for all, luckily in a separate little building away from the house. There was always a queue outside it, usually because the major was soaking himself inside, while Mrs Fetlock interrogated him about the farm accounts. It was the only place where she could pin him down to do this; there were too many outstanding bills, which he preferred not to think about.

The Major possessed a peppery temper, and the Africans who worked for him were terrified of him. And when he lost patience with them and became heated, a not infrequent occurrence, like rabbits caught in the headlights, they lost their wits and became accident prone.

My mother welcomed the prospect of riding again; her fox-hunting father had taught her to ride as a child. So, one afternoon soon after we had settled in, she set off on one of the horses for a good long outing, unaware that her eldest son was following on foot. He, aged eight, was quite unable to keep up with the horse, but doggedly kept trotting after it until she disappeared into the distance, whereupon he became lost. My mother returned in the late afternoon, to find he had disappeared. The Major was approached, a crisis was proclaimed, and he took military control. Platoons of Africans were rounded up and sent off to search in every direction.

"When the Piccanniny Baas is found," he instructed his search parties before they departed, "I shall fire my Makuru Makuru (big, big) gun to tell you."

The sound of the booming reverberations of his elephant gun resounding round the kopjies surrounding the homestead and triumphantly announcing the discovery of my brother still echo in my ears.

Another memory is of Major Fetlock taking me, now aged three, for a ride on James Pigge, his horse. He had a withered left arm as a result of his war wounds. With this arm I was held in a Napoleonic grasp against his chest once I was set in front of him.

"Mind the brute", roared the Major as my mother handed me up onto the horse, "he bites at one end and kicks at the other!" James Pigge, his charger, cavorting and showing the whites of his eyes, was then spurred into an exhilarating gallop.

"Young feller didn't seem scared," he said, when I was returned to a rather pale mother. I don't recall ever being allowed to ride with him again.

The bathroom had a boiler similar to that built by my father. It too had to be filled by hand with buckets of water, which had to be carried a long way. With paying guests now accommodated by the Fetlocks, the boiler needed constant refilling if all were to have a bath. There was an additional feature to the Fetlock bathroom; the waste water emptied into a large drum sunk into the ground outside, so that it could be reused to water the tomatoes grown nearby. With so many guests, the bathroom queue was often long, and on one particular evening my mother and I were last in the queue. While we were waiting I heard a leopard coughing in one of the kopjies nearby. When we at last got in, and the hot tap was turned on, there was a soapy gurgle, and a mixture like frothy grey soup gushed into the bath. The African responsible for refilling the boiler decided that, if he reused the water intended for the tomatoes, it would save a lot of effort carrying buckets of fresh water from the far distant source. So he had refilled the boiler from the waste drum. My mother complained, interrupting Major Fetlock's sundowner, and he went rampaging off into the dusk, only to find that the African responsible had prudently disappeared.

Major Fetlock acquired considerable notoriety in the district. Cissie recounted his exploits to her friends with gusto. They provided much needed light relief in the darker days of the war. Many of his problems were of his own making. He expected too much from his Africans, treating them as he had no doubt treated the soldiers in his old regiment. He was unwise enough to ask them to do such jobs as filling up the petrol tank of his car, even after several times it ran out of petrol. This was not something to be endured happily by a man possessed of very little patience as passing vehicles which could provide assistance were infrequent on Rhodesian roads. But, with a long journey to Salisbury in prospect, he one day again told one of the Africans to " fill her up." Later that evening he saw the same man and enquired if his orders had been carried out.

"Yah Baas. Aikona Baas." quavered the African, hedging his bets with 'yes' and 'no' in the same sentence, not a good reply to a man who expected concise answers.

"Well go and see, you skellum!" he roared, and stumped off rumbling. It was dusk, so the terrified African hurried off to the kitchen for a light. Now it is not the best way to check whether there is any petrol in a car to use a lighted match to look in the tank. The car was wrecked. Somehow the African survived, but no longer in the Major's employment, much to the relief of both.

Soon after this the Major went to the local railway station to collect a new paying guest. On the platform waiting for him he found a lady of considerable bulk.

"It's a good thing that I brought the truck", was his welcoming remark.

The farmhouse hygiene was not good, and I began to suffer from stomach upsets. My mother decided it was time to move. She found a cottage, originally built for a farm manager, on another farm near Salisbury. This she rented for the rest of the war.

Chapter 14. A monkey and a Thunderstorm.

The cottage into which we moved was on a tobacco farm, twenty miles from Salisbury. There was a railway siding nearby with the very English name of Melfort. The owner of the farm was Southern Irish, so felt no obligation to join up. Their farmhouse was not far from the cottage so we saw a little of them. His wife spent most of her time on a sofa with her Pekinese. Outside their house roamed a pack of spaniels which were not permitted indoors: they barked at anything and at anybody, but particularly at small boys. A pet baboon was also kept. Baboons may have some attraction when very young which I have been unable to discern, but when they grow up they develop fearsome teeth and unattractive habits. This baboon was kept chained to a tree at the back of the house where the Africans, from a safe distance, teased it. Not surprisingly it detested the human race. To keep it company a vervet monkey was also tied up beside it. The monkey received much the same treatment from the Africans as the baboon, but being cleverer, soon found out how to escape.

My first acquaintance with it was when it crept up behind me when I was innocently drawing on our verandah, and bit me in my ankle. The bite turned septic, and I was taken to Salisbury hospital for treatment. The hospital was staffed by nuns. They inspected the wound and my mother asked what they intended to do.

"We shall cauterise it," they said.

My mother, being a doctor's daughter, knew what this would entail, but thought that although a red hot iron would undoubtedly sterilise every known bug in Africa, it was too drastic a remedy for her five year old son. So she took me away unseared and prepared an old fashioned poultice from a mixture of glycerine and Epsom salts. This drew out the poison successfully, although I still carry a scar.

The monkey's reign of terror continued. It crept up on me again later when I was making mud pies, and bit me on my arm. On another occasion it followed my brother and I on his bicycle, he being old enough now to put me on his carrier, all the way to a neighbour's farm. When we saw it we took refuge in their swimming pool, and refused to come out until it had been chased off. The final insult came when it got into our pantry and was discovered making paw marks on my newly iced birthday cake.

The baboon came to our rescue. Somehow its chain became wound around the monkey's neck when they were tied up together, and the monkey was garroted. It did not occur to me that the baboon may have disliked the monkey just as much as we did until this attractive possibility was suggested by my brother. But this became the only occasion on which I have ever felt grateful to a baboon.

There were wartime shortages in Southern Rhodesia just as there were in England, although not as severe. Milk, butter, eggs and meat were all freely available for us. But flour was still imported, so Rhodesian wartime bread contained maize meal. I did not encounter proper white bread until I was in hospital later with malaria; I thought it delicious. Toys were virtually unobtainable, but this was no great hardship, as my mother made stuffed animals for me out of scrap materials, often with whiskers of real horsehair. And I created my own with the resources available. My bed, for example, became a realistic sailing ship once I had unfurled the mosquito net to make a sail, and I set out on many a perilous excursion to treasure islands, or against dastardly pirates once my ship was rigged and manned with a doughty crew of stuffed animals.

The chief worry was petrol, since our ration was eight gallons a month. As the weekly shopping required a round trip of forty miles, not much was left for other events such as social calls, particularly as our Irish neighbours frequently came calling with rubber tubing and cans to borrow some by siphoning it out of our tank.

On trips to Salisbury my mother quickly learnt the trick of making the most of her ration. At the top of every well remembered hill the car's engine would be switched off and it would coast down in neutral, with creaks and groans from the protesting bodywork. At the bottom of the hill the clutch would be let out with a jerk, and with a roar the engine would restart to haul us up the next incline. In town visits would be made to the Standard Bank, post office, butcher and grocer. A call was then essential to 'Pockets' for my mother to revive herself with tea, and I would be given a 'Knicker-Bocker Glory', a tall glass containing tinned fruit- salad topped with ice cream and a glace cherry. For a while the world had nothing better to offer me. Visits might follow to Kingston's, or Ness & Archibald, the two booksellers in the town.

On the next- door farm was another ex-serviceman wounded in the first world war. He, like my father, had been in the Royal Flying Corps, and had lost a leg but thereby gained a pension. The prospect of a warmer climate and cheap land had drawn him to Rhodesia, as it had many other ex-service men. I don't remember much farming taking place on his farm, but it provided a comfortable house with a swimming pool, and grazing for his horses. With his background in the R.F.C. he entertained some of the Royal Air Force personnel who were being trained in the colony, so there was a constant flow of young men staying on leave there. There were also two young daughters of about the same age as my brother and I, who were thought by our mother to be good for us, as they enabled us to meet other children with whom we had not had much contact before. My brother and I did not agree; girls, we learnt, were unpredictable, and could be bossy too. Further away lived the Cullinan family. Rumour had it that Mr. Cullinan was related to the finder of the famous Cullinan diamond, the largest ever discovered and now part of the crown jewels. Rumour may or may not have been correct, but the neighbourhood believed Mr Cullinan to be fabulously rich so when they entertained their neighbours descended on them like locusts to devour all on offer. The Cullinans gave a tennis party shortly after one Christmas, perhaps forgetting that this occurred during the middle of the wet season. To get to their house it was necessary to cross a river, the crossing being made over 'drift'. This was a flat area of concrete laid on the bed of the river: the level of water running over it did not normally exceed two or three inches, so cars could usually drive across without difficulty.

A large number of guests duly arrived for the tennis and all went well until the sky, which had been blackening amid ominous grumbles of thunder all afternoon, suddenly opened and torrents of rain fell. Tennis was abruptly terminated, and the grownups retired indoors for a "gin or two". The Cullinans were generous hosts and it wasn't until an hour or more later that guests with young children started to leave. They were soon back. The drift was now covered by a roaring flood and was quite impassable. There was no other way out, so the Cullinans were stuck with their tennis guests for the night. Nothing daunted, more food and drinks were found, and soon the roar and turbulence among the adults exceeded that of the flood over the drift. At last beds or sofas were found for the ladies, and rugs with cushions or car seats for the young, while the men made a night of it over the whisky. Next morning a succession of cars carrying sleepy children and quarrelling adults crept home across the now fordable drift, but whatever their condition, the party afterwards became a legend.

Chapter 15. Lake Nyasa and Malaria.

We stayed at this cottage for the rest of the war. My mother struggled with her African staff; she never learnt much of their language and had insufficient patience to train them, so they carried out only basic work such as sweeping, chopping wood and washing up. The houseboy was a dilapidated old body called Ticket, who went around in a daze with bloodshot eyes all day. It was only later that I was told that he must have been a smoker of 'dagga', the local maruanja. There was also a piccanin, whose main job was to chop wood and bring it in to the kitchen for the Dover wood stove. He soon decided that it was far easier to steal the already chopped wood from next door than to chop it himself. This was discovered and Mr. Simmonds came roaring over in an Irish fury and caned him over the kitchen table until pitiful cries of "mi wei, mi wei" were heard. This left a distinctly chilly atmosphere between the households; whereas a similar punishment would have been given to my brother or myself at school for such an offence, my parents would never have done such a thing to an African. It was also illegal. A letter from my mother to my father a few weeks after this reads:-

"Dear Maurice, I got your letter from Moshi…How they do dodge you about! I now have a new piccanin to work in the garden, a relation of Ticket's. He seems to do twice as much as the last half grown villain, if not more. The last one was a thief. I'm sure he stole some kitchen knives and several small articles besides, including my umbrella! But have no means of proving it. I hope you are now settled in, with not too bad company…"

When I was five, we went on a 'seaside' holiday. Only it wasn't beside the sea, it was beside Lake Nyasa. As I could not see land on the far horizon it was, as far as I was concerned, a sea; the lack of salt in the water did not matter. The journey to get there, through parts of Africa that were still virtually uninhabited by Europeans, was almost more exciting for my brother and I than the holiday once we had arrived.

A car with an African driver was hired for part of the journey. This was unusual, as there were very few Africans able and allowed to drive cars then. The road was daunting, being little more than a dirt-track hacked through the bush. There were few bridges, and I recall two river crossings over large rivers were made by driving the car onto a pontoon, which was then pulled across to the other side by Africans heaving on a rope from the opposite bank. Part of what was then Portuguese East Africa had to be crossed, so passports were needed at the borders. In my baggage was 'Sydney', my bear, so named because he came from Australia and was a koala. He had been provided by my ever inventive parent with his own passport, complete with a graphic portrait. A British Customs Officer, dressed in immaculate white uniform, seeing me with my bear enquired jovially if the bear had a passport. To his astonishment, I produced one which, after it had been carefully inspected, he stamped. I was very proud of my bear after that.

We had to stay a night en route in Tete, a Portuguese town on the banks of the Zambezi. The river here was extremely broad, and the town had a fort, rather like the one in the Beau Geste film. This made it seem a very exciting place.

The following morning our car was driven onto another pontoon. A steam- launch was attached to this to tow it across the great Zambezi. We got into the launch for the crossing, to find that on its deck lay an elephant gun.

"What's that for?" we asked, to be told that it was to protect us if we were attacked by hippos. My brother and I were deeply disappointed when no attack occurred; my mother was less so.

Once safely across, we drove on North through the seemingly never ending African bush. We met a troop of baboons crossing the road. I never liked baboons, but I was deeply upset when our driver deliberately ran over one. At last we reached Blantyre.

The last part of our journey was made by train, pulled by a wood fired steam locomotive. This was very slow and the day became increasingly hot. I became grumpy and so disagreeable that my brother eventually thumped me. In doing so he unfortunately knocked out one of my teeth, which gave me the excuse to make a hideous din. All the blame thereupon descended upon him. The eldest brother's lot is not a happy one.

At our 'seaside' resort we went on boat excursions on the lake, fished and swam. I picked up a crocodile's tooth on the beach which became a treasured possession and later saw a large pair of nostrils swimming past - a hippo, not a crocodile, I was told. Close to the hotel was an inlet in which there were dugout canoes, used by the local Africans to go out fishing. On the day we left we were asked by one of them if we would like to go with them; due to our forthcoming departure we had to say no, but I have always regretted that the invitation came too late.

On our return journey the car developed problems, and we had to make an unscheduled stop in a Portuguese settlement, where we spent the night in a dirty little hotel. The mosquito nets over the beds were old and grubby and had many holes which let in the mosquitoes.

Three weeks later I was delirious, trying to climb the wall by my bed and crying out that there were leopards chasing me. I can remember seeing myself doing this from a place outside my body, and being aware of my distraught mother trying to calm me at the same time. I had contracted a severe case of malaria. An unpleasant three weeks in hospital followed; my head constantly buzzing as a result of the quinine with which I was being stuffed. The nuns who nursed me were the same ones who had said they would cauterise my infected monkey bite a year before; they gave me humiliating enemas and were an unsympathetic lot. I have had a hatred of hospitals ever since. I came out feeling very shaky and it was months before I was fully fit. For some years after the malaria would recur from time to time.

Chapter 16. Boarding School.

The end of the war brought changes in my life. The first was the return of my father. After five years and three hundred and four days of service in the Army, he was released on 28th September, 1945 'in consequence of the demobilisation', with the rank of Captain. He was exhausted. He was now 51, and had served his country throughout the whole of two world wars. For these he received six campaign medals. He was proudest of the 1914 Star, and his R.F.C. Observer's badge.

He was given sixty one days leave at the end of the war. I assume he received some sort of gratuity when he left, but he received no pension. He kept his service revolver, which I think was careless of the army.

Just before he returned, I went to boarding school. I was just eight. I went to Ruzawi, which my brother had just left. This move was a shock. I was thrown from the cozy security of my home into an alien world ruled by time tables and bells, and I had not yet learnt to tell the time - there had been no need to do so up until then. Moreover, there was no privacy at school. Bathrooms and lavatories with no doors were shared by all the boys, and matron daily asked you unsettling questions about the state of your bowels which shocked and disgusted me.

Ruzawi School was, looking back, a very good school. When I went on to one of the best known schools in South Africa later, I, and other boys from Ruzawi, were two years ahead of most of those of our age from South African schools. The Board of Governors for Ruzawi included both the Governor and the Bishop of Rhodesia. The school buildings were superb, having been built in the Dutch colonial style, with an endowment from the Alfred Beit Trust, in grounds of 700 acres. The Headmaster was a clergyman with a degree from Oxford. He had one glass eye, as a result of a war wound. I never knew quite which eye this was. I found him quite terrifying most of the time, and the only person more frightened of him was, I discovered much later, my mother. He believed in discipline of the old fashioned variety, and never spoilt a child by sparing the rod.

I discovered this quite early, for passing his study one day I heard the vicious whistle and crack of his cane, and a friend of mine came out bawling like a calf while rubbing his behind. I decided from that moment on that I should become very inconspicuous.

Alas, good intentions are soon forgotten. Only a few days later, who should suddenly find himself still without one sock on and alone in a suddenly all too quiet dormitory. And, coming to his senses, wailing to himself,

"Oh, crikey! I shall be late for morning roll call, and the Whole School will see!"

The junior dormitory was at one end of the building; at the other end of a long cloister was the assembly area. 'Bang!' went the dormitory door behind me as I tore off along that terrible long cloister. At the end of it was the staff room. Round the corner I shot, and whom should I meet in a head-on collision but an African bearing a tray on which was early morning tea for the entire teaching staff. There was the most appalling smashing, crashing and tinkling, as cups, saucers, spoons, teapot and hot water flew everywhere, followed by an even more appalling shocked silence, as the whole school did indeed see.

"Now I am really for it," I thought.

But someone came to my rescue. The first concern for the African, that most kind and wonderful man, was not for the staff tea, nor the smashed crockery, nor even for the hot water splashed over his bare feet, but for me.

"Baas, Piccaninny Baas, wena O.K.?" (are you all right?), he asked, going down on his hands and knees to pick me up. Who could have dared to punish me after his concern?

I settled down. I could read well; I was generally nearer the top of the class than the bottom, and my early reports show me first in Art, Nature Study and Scripture. The first two subjects were undoubtedly due to the interest fostered by my mother, but the last amazes me, as it was not a subject with which I had been much acquainted before. I can only assume it was in my genes, as there were many parsons among the Greenhows, Petches and Peaches who were my forebears.

Weekly letters from my mother were a great comfort, and Matron soon began to enjoy them as much as I did. She read them to me during the afternoon rest period, because I had difficulty reading my mother's hand writing, which was always appalling. Her letters were usually illustrated, and often ostensibly sent by one of our animals. Patrick O'Growler, our Irish terrier, was soon sending me accounts of his fictional 'posh' school, complete with complaints about it very similar to those I was probably putting in my letters home. Patrick was, as might be expected, always in trouble at school and wanted to leave, but the exploits which got him into trouble had Matron and me in fits of giggles. The letters were later turned into a short story which was broadcasted on Rhodesian Radio's equivalent of 'Children's Hour ', but when I received them they did a lot to help me cope with my new life away from home.

Patrick O'growler receiving his medicine at school
(Illustration from my mother's story)

Meanwhile my parents were planning to go back to the farm. My father must either have felt that, as he was now fifty one, it was too late for him to do anything else, or that if he was eventually to sell the farm it must be brought back to a working condition first. It had stood empty and uncared for throughout the war. I do not think that my mother returned to it with much enthusiasm, but farming had prospered during the war, and after it the number of farmers in the district was increasing. So, loyally and stoically, she went back with him.

It was during the long holiday from school at Christmas that I first returned. My parents must have just started to prepare the house for reoccupation, as I remember supper being cooked over an open fire in the dining room, with virtually no furniture to sit on or eat off. That night I slept on a camp bed in front of the dying embers, and went to sleep thinking how exciting life was now going to be during my holidays in future.

Chapter 17. Back to the Farm.

I went back to school while my parents were putting the farm back to life. During the period it had stood empty a veldt fire had swept through the 'gum' plantation, but eucalyptus are sturdy trees, and they had revived.

A local Dutch farmer told us that there was a leopard living on Ruanda which had taken several of his calves. It killed one of our bullocks later, which added a frisson to my life, although I never saw this one until later. Leopards were still quite common, but were frequently shot by farmers, as they tended to prey upon livestock as this one had done. I remember a professional hunter bringing the carcass of one that he had shot to my school so that we boys could admire it. In addition to our leopard there was a large pack of baboons moving destructively around, in spite of its' presence. Leopards would eat a baboon if they could catch one.

Dead Leopard.

The farm house had squatters. A swarm of wild bees had taken over the roof space above the main bedroom. And squirrels had taken up residence in the remainder of the house, like the stoats and weasels in Kenneth Graham's Toad Hall, I thought. The squirrels were easily evicted, although they drove our dogs quite frantic by making rude noises at them from the safety of the rafters and the surrounding trees. This I learnt from another of the graphic illustrations which were sent to me in my mother's letters.

The bees however, proved to be more of a problem, since they were difficult to reach , and ferocious when disturbed. My father told my mother not to fuss. But every day several dozen bees would drop down into the bedroom. My father would squash a few with a matchbox against a window pane when passing, and my mother would spray the room with a 'Flit' spray, shut the door and retire elsewhere. But she got stung from time to time, and eventually the house boy refused to sweep the floor after being stung on his bare foot. No positive action took place until a somnolent bee crawled its way into one of Dad's shoes, and came to life vengefully when trodden on. This finally provoked him into doing something. A porous old stocking was filled with DDT powder and tied onto the end of a long gum pole. The stocking was then shaken vigorously, from the safety of the distant pantry which had no ceiling, over the hive. The bees exploded into action with an angry roar, the gum pole was hastily flung down, and the bedroom ceiling collapsed under its' horrid weight of dead bees, honey- comb and dirt into the bedroom beneath. The honey alas, could not be eaten, being contaminated by the DDT.

At the end of my school term, I returned to a rejuvenated farmhouse. I was now eight, and my brother Kenneth was fourteen. We both had bicycles, and began to explore the district together. We were given complete freedom, and went wherever and as far as we wanted. Mealtimes provided a good incentive to be home on time.

On the other side of the railway line was land unsuitable for farming, scattered with rocks and kopjies. It received no attention from its owner, a reclusive Dutchman, whom we seldom met. We roamed this area unchallenged.

The nearest kopjie there was of special interest because on it was a cave containing Bushman Paintings. The Bushmen had long since been ousted from Rhodesia by the local Bantu tribes to other less fertile parts of Africa, but in many places they left behind a poignant record of their life, depicted in their delicate red ochre paintings. These survived on the rocks where they had been painted, inside caves or on concave rocks where the paintings were sheltered from the sun and rain. Those near us showed sticklike men, with the prominent buttocks characteristic of their race, carrying bows, arrows and spears, together with a woman with a bundle on her head. Alongside were animals which had not been seen in the district for decades, such as giraffe and sable antelope. Nearby, beside delicately drawn trees and shaded rocks, stalked a lifelike secretary bird, with the 'quill' behind his ear plain to see.

Bushman paintings copied by Cissie

Further away was a much larger kopjie. This contained two gigantic granite rock formations. One we named 'the Ship Rock', since it resembled the prow of a ship. The other, which stood well over one hundred feet high, became 'Baboon Castle'.

My brother Kenneth was now an expert on birds. From an early age he had been encouraged to keep a nature diary, which I still possess. In this, by the time he was nine, he had recorded, drawn and water coloured no less than thirty four different species, with exotic names such as:-

Orange Throated Long Claw
Purple- crested Lourie
Water Dikkop
Knob Billed Duck
Spotted Eagle Owl
Paradise Fly Catcher
Blue Waxbill
Clapper Lark
Drongo
Hammerkop
Kurrichane Thrush.

He collected eggs, taking only one egg from a nest, and then only if others were present. The eggs he collected were drilled with neat holes made with discarded dental drills which he begged from a dentist, and then blown dry. He often carried a distinct smell of fresh egg on his person. Many birds nested on ledges on the rocks, and since baboons were great nest robbers, birds learnt to build in very inaccessible places to survive. Not many humans can out climb a baboon without special equipment such as ropes. My brother had not yet acquired such luxuries, but the incentive to reach inaccessible nests turned him into a very proficient climber without them.

Baboon Castle had a narrow cleft running up its center, and Kenneth it was who taught me how to 'chimney' up clefts by pressing my back against one side with my hands and feet, and forcing my way up it foot by foot with my feet.

Baboon Castle

Alone there one day I decided I was going to climb to the top, a thing that I had never done before. Leaving Dad's old .22 rifle guarded by the dogs at the bottom, up I went until I reached the top of the cleft where, with a twist and a scramble, I arrived at the summit. The sky was a cloudless blue, and it seemed as if all Africa lay below me. From North to South the dark ribbon of the railway line stretched away to each horizon like one of those black millipedes that looped their way round our garden in the wet season. To the East the thousand acres of Chigwani Farm lay spread out with house, African quarters, paddocks, plantations, avenues and crops all visible. Ruanda kopjie lowered behind, crowned with the eucalyptus trees planted by my father. At last, coming back to earth, I looked down from my eyrie. Two ant sized dogs were beginning to fret and whine below.

"Time to get down", I thought. And then, "Oh Lord! how ?"

It is not too difficult to climb a cleft of the right width by jamming yourself in at the bottom and working your way up. It is a different matter when you find yourself looking down a one hundred foot drop, are alone, and realize that somehow you have to throw yourself across it and clamp your back to one wall with your feet on the other, and there is nothing to hold onto while you do it. How I did it I cannot recall, but I do remember that it took a long time before I attempted it.

"Well", said the dogs, leaping up and down to meet me at the bottom, "we thought you were never going to come down!".

"And so, for a while, did I", I told them. But I never told my parents.

It was a good thing that they never knew all that their sons got up to while out.

Chapter 18. Butter and Storms.

"Come, butter, come! Come, butter come! Oh, it's so hot! Can you have a go now?"

There was a rumble of thunder in the distance as my mother passed me the butter churn. It was hot and sultry. I was back from school for the long Christmas holiday, which was also the season for rain. The corrugated iron roof of the house creaked and groaned as it expanded and contracted with the changes of heat, the clouds rolled over the sky , and the sun came and went in between them.

"The butter never seems to come in this weather," said my mother, "in winter the cream needs hardly any churning before it appears".

I vigorously wound the handle on top of the churn which turned the paddles inside. The cream, which had risen to the surface of the milk previously left standing in a wide bowl in the cool of the pantry, had been skimmed off and put into the churn. The skim milk was retained separately until it soured, when it was made into cream cheese.

At last the butter appeared in its sudden mysterious way. It was placed on a sloping board where my mother slapped, prodded and flattened it with two wooden grooved butter pats, washing it with clean water from a jug the while. After a final flattening, it was salted and fashioned into its final rolls, each patterned by the grooves on the butter pats. Meanwhile the dark clouds had been rolling up, and the lightning flashes and peals of thunder had been getting nearer. At lunch we ate cold beef.

"This animal must have come out of the Ark with Noah", said my mother, chewing the leathery meat.

There was another flash, a boom of thunder, and the opening patter of heavy raindrops on the iron roof, which soon turned into a steady roar as the storm broke, until the hammering became so loud that conversation was impossible. Yet by the time lunch was finished the worst was over.

"Would you like a hand or two of whist with me, little man?" asked my father, and we retreated to the sitting room. He liked to relax for a while after lunch; it was too hot for farm work in the middle of the day, and he was a very early riser.

"You have the luck of the devil", he said as my face betrayed that I had picked up another fat trump, but he still managed to win the odd trick at the end of the game. He had had a great deal of time to learn how, when he was a prisoner of war.

Outside the sun came out, and the grateful earth breathed out promise of fresh growth.

"Should have done the maize some good," said my father, as he strode off back to work.

Chapter 19. Africans and Language

Farm life gave me greater contact with Africans, and I learnt to speak more fluently with them. Rhodesia had many different tribes within its borders, and they all spoke different languages. Workers also came down from Nyasaland with their own dialect. So a bastard common language for all had evolved, a mixture of Africaans, English and African words, which was called 'Kitchen Kaffir'. It now goes by the politer description of 'Chilapalapa'. I soon got to know it quite well.

Many white children on farms were looked after by African nannies, and some of these children spoke better Chilapalapa than English when young. I used to find it a great joke when I sometimes heard the most appalling African swear words issuing from the lips of angelic looking white infants, their mothers remaining blissfully ignorant the while. They had, of course, learnt these words while with their African nannies. House boys and other male African staff often spent their idle hours flirting with, or trying to seduce the nannies, and it was probably when 'nanny' was fending off such attentions that the choicer words were passed on to the children with them.

The English sense of humour often found its

way into Kitchen Kaffir, which led to unfortunate misunderstandings. For example, Englishmen sometimes referred to hens as 'm'faazis', although the correct meaning of 'm'faazi' was 'married woman', and the common word for a hen was 'huku'. But the English thought that the chattering and high pitched laughter when a group of African women were together was very like the noise of a hen house, and so hens became 'm'faazis'. But, although they would have enjoyed the joke, African males were not let in on it, and when the cook was told to:- "humba bulala munya m'faazi", when a chicken was wanted for dinner, literally translated the order meant, "go and kill one wife". No wonder they thought white people were mad.

The Makonis in our district were a feckless lot. Saturday and Sunday nights were spent dancing and drinking 'wa wa', their home brewed beer. Many a night I lay awake, listening to the dim drums throbbing, and the singing in the distance. On Monday morning, a queue of 'boys' soliciting medicine from the 'N'kosikaas' was a regular occurrence. On being asked what was the matter, they would clutch their heads, or rub their bellies, proclaiming sadly that they had "Nyoka lapa", meaning "a snake down here". I thought that a snake writhing in one's belly was a graphic way of describing a tummy ache, but my unsympathetic parent's response was usually to administer a large dose of Epsom salts. Medicines dispensed on the farm had to be administered daily under supervision. If an African was given a bottle of castor oil and told to take a spoonful every day, he would return the following day, if he was able to, with an empty bottle. Like British sailors, they believed that 'more was better'. The medicine from the empty bottle would be described with a mournful, but admiring, shake of the head as being "steric, meningi steric". (Strong, very strong).A few basic remedies were kept on the farm for emergencies; Dettol, bandages, aspirin, quinine, castor oil. Serious cases were few, and taken to the hospital in Rusape when necessary

African workers, hard at work sawing gum poles.

One gruesome day my brother found a dead body. It was that of an African who had died by hanging. This had occurred some considerable time before Kenneth found the remains, since the rope had rotted and the body was on the ground. The police came, and my father was told that suicide was the cause. The dead man had worn good clothes, and still had coins in his pockets. Suicide was not uncommon among Africans, the policeman told us, particularly if a man believed he had been cursed by a witch doctor. The young policeman's rueful remark to my father after a gruesome morning's work was:-

"If your son ever finds another dead body, can he manage not to do so on a Sunday!"

Africans sometimes came down all the way from Nyasaland to work in Rhodesia. There were fewer Europeans farms in their country, so work was less easy to find there. They came on government contracts, usually for one or two years. My father preferred them to the locals, as they were more responsible and hard- working, and often saved their wages with him until they returned home. We had a Head Man who came from Nyasaland who had a natural dignity; in spite of being a foreigner he was respected by all.

The locals, as well as being frequently drunk at weekends, were gamblers. They played a game called T'soro, in which stones or 'Lucky Beans' (the red and black seeds of the Erithythrina tree) were moved about singly or in groups in holes formed on a board or a rock, or even in the sand. I would watch while large bets were made during these games, which were played with many a disappointed grunt or triumphant shout .

On a nearby farm there was a carpenter's shop where an old and skilled African worked on his own. I used to go and watch him – a far more interesting way of passing the time than listening to boring grownup talk. And it was from him that I heard tales of Kalulu, the clever hare who always outwits other animals. Kalulu was the original source for 'Br'er Rabbit' in the Uncle

Remus fables published in America, transported thither by Africans taken for slaves to the plantations in the South.

My favourite Kalulu story was that involving Hyena, who stole from a village a goat, a leopard and a basket of meal. He ran away with them until he reached the wide river where he had left his canoe in which he planned to escape. Alas, the canoe was not big enough for himself and all his booty.

"Oh, Kalulu, what shall I do, cried Hyena, "if I take the goat and the leopard across the river and leave them there, the leopard will eat the goat while I return for the basket. And if I take the goat and the basket, the goat will eat the meal while I paddle back for the leopard. Tell me what to do, Kalulu."

"Easy," said Kalulu, "take the leopard and the goat across the river first. Tie up the goat on the far bank , and then return with the leopard still in your canoe to pick up the basket".

"How clever!" said Hyena, and set off across the river with the leopard and the goat. But when he returned for the basket he found that both Kalulu and the basket had gone. Kalulu had taken the opportunity to steal the basket of meal while Hyena was on the other side of the river.

Chapter 20. Cattle Dipping.

On Monday mornings lowing and bellowing was heard from the paddock. The cattle were being rounded up. The paddock was an area of several hundred acres in front of the house enclosed by a barbed wire fence. Within it, as well as the grass which grew up to six foot tall in places in the wet season, were many rocky outcrops and small kopjies covered with trees, which made it unsuitable for cultivation.

The herd contained around a hundred beef animals, and were ruled by a lordly old Red Poll bull. They roamed wild and free most of the time, but each week during the 'tick' season they had to be put through the cattle dip.

This meant total immersion in an evil smelling greenish coloured chemical mix which kept them free of ticks. If not dipped they became infested with these parasites which they picked up from the long grass, and which attached themselves to their ears and other soft skinned areas. Dogs and humans were also vulnerable; many an hour I spent pulling these horrible swollen blue parasites from the dogs, as the preventative treatments now available could not be obtained then. Ticks transmitted disease through their bites; even in gentle England now humans can get Lyme's Disease from a tick bite.

I enjoyed dipping, for it was noisy work, full of dust

and drama, providing a welcome change to quieter days. The dip had been built by my father before the war. With its angled walls, steps, sloping bottom and long draining pen, it had been far more difficult to build than the farmhouse, he said. It was just wide enough to allow one beast to go through at a time, was deep enough to make that animal swim through it, and it sloped up to the exit where each animal would scramble out.

The cattle were driven through in batches; once each batch was through, it stood for a while in the draining pen to allow the liquid to drip off and run back into the dip.

At the entrance stood my father, on a side step and armed with a long pole, in the forefront of the battle. It was not a pleasant place to be as when each animal jumped in there was a tremendous splash, which produced a nauseous shower for anyone too close. But he would not delegate the job to anyone else.

"Dip, dip, dip! we shouted, whacking and pushing the cattle towards the entrance, while the bellowing and moaning of the herd rose to a crescendo. Standing on the brink, every animal teetered awhile with rolling eyes and flaring nostrils, trying to avoid the dreaded plunge.

"Dip, Dip, Dip! the shouts grew louder, until the pressure from the animals behind forced the front one to jump, with a thunderous splash, into the vile bath. Old animals would hold their heads high and close their eyes as they went in; younger bullocks and calves would go in bawling, and rise choking, until they had learnt to keep their mouths shut. Each animal would be ducked by my father using the long pole, if its head had not gone under, as it was essential for the liquid to protect their delicate ears.

Once each batch was through and drying in the draining pen, calm would descend.

The Africans would gather to joke and laugh together, " mushlie sabenze, heh", (soft work this!). They liked working with cattle. Once they had dried, the batch of animals standing there would be released into a larger holding area, the gate to the draining area closed behind it and the drama would recommence, until all were dipped and dry.

The other job I enjoyed watching was when the herd was fed with rock salt. There was a lack of salt in the earth, and the cattle loved to lick the great lumps given them to remedy this deficiency. There was never any need to call them, they came running, bellowing with anticipation, as soon as they saw my father. He generally did this towards the evening, and it was pleasant to stand by the fence, watching the cattle jostling, licking and finally when they had had enough salt, contentedly settling down to chewing the cud, while the air cooled and softened, the sun went down, and an occasional night jar purred afar off as night tiptoed in.

Chapter 21. Contrasting lives - School and Farm.

I now had two separate and very different lives. For eight months I led a disciplined life at boarding school; for the remaining four I roamed the veld and lived as wild and free as I liked on the farm.

At the end of each holiday my mother would put me on the train for school, each of us silent with misery. School terms were a desolate time for her, as there was less company on the farm while her children were away. She usually collected me from school when, Oh Frabjous day, term ended. The end of term coincided with some sort of event for parents, such as sports day or a school play, and gave her a pretext for getting away from the farm. If she did not come, I returned on the train, counting off the little halts and villages with their curious mixture of African and English names all the way - Tarasira, Theydon, Macheke, Umfeseri, Eagle's Nest, Headlands; the train seemed to crawl between them going home, as it stopped at each place to load and unload mail bags and parcels, milk churns and the occasional passenger, until at last, caloo, calay! unlovely Baddeley Siding came in sight, with its ugly Ganger's cottage, scrubby m'sasa trees, parcel store and concrete platform, where my parents would be waiting to take me home to an ecstatic welcome from the dogs.

School life went on around a strict timetable. Mr. Grinham, the Headmaster, believed that if boys were kept busy, there was less opportunity for them to get into mischief, so we worked or played throughout the day, six days a week. The staff were kept as busy as we were; most were unmarried, all lived in the school. When not teaching, they would be attending chapel with us, or supervising games, prep., or other activities, such as rehearsing the school play, or the Scouts or Cubs. They even attended our P.T. classes, which usually meant they did the exercises too! Most of them enjoyed it and thrived; those that did not left quickly and unlamented.

Our day started with a shower or a dip in the swimming pool (naked), followed by roll call, cocoa, chapel, P.T. and prep. By breakfast time we had a keen appetite. Visits were then made to Sister, if ailments need treatment, or the Headmaster, if ordered. An interview with the Headmaster following some misdemeanour often ended with a very painful caning.

Assembly came next, with lessons after. A half hour's morning break included cricket or football practice, with an orange or some pea nuts for refreshment after, before more lessons, which included Latin for the older boys. A rest was taken after lunch, followed by lessons every afternoon except Wednesdays and Saturdays, when games were obligatory. The day concluded with supper, more prep., chapel and bed.

On Sundays we dressed in Boy Scout or Cub uniforms, and wrote letters home after morning chapel instead of doing P.T. and prep. After breakfast the whole school paraded on three sides of a square round the flag pole, faced by the Headmaster, dressed in immaculate Scout uniform and Baden Powell hat, and the Union Jack was raised with military ceremony, three senior Scouts forming a 'colour party', and marching with the rolled union jack up to the flag pole to attach and hoist it. Once raised, the Headmaster pulled the lower rope attached to the flag to 'break out' the colours, and we all saluted. When I later went to the Britannia Royal Naval College at Dartmouth, the routine there was very similar!

Parents could take their children out for the day on Sundays. Friends would be invited, and a picnic taken to favourite sites nearby. The rest of the school went for walks in the surrounding bush, accompanied by a member of staff, until lunchtime. No boy was ever allowed to sleep away from school during term time.

The school was surrounded by seven hundred acres of its own land. Tall Eucalyptus trees surrounded the playing fields and grounds. The chapel was a plain white washed building with a thatched roof. It had been a cow shed in former times, when there had been a Coaching Inn on the site which had been on the old Umtali to Salisbury road before the railway was built. Near the main entrance to the school was a cemetery, in which were the graves of several settlers killed during the Mashona uprising which broke out in the 1890s. Each year Mr Grinham conducted an open air memorial service there, with the whole school solemnly standing around their graves. The school had been founded in 1928, and a number of its old boys died serving in the British Forces in the Second World War. Their names were read out in Chapel on Remembrance Day.

The atmosphere was of pride in, and loyalty to the British Empire. During history lessons we regarded with awe maps of the world showing the vast areas coloured red which still were part the Empire - Canada, Australia,

New Zealand, and of course, large swathes of Africa, including our own. Rhodesian sentiments regarding the British Empire were twenty years behind those of dis-enchanted post-war Britain I found when I went to England later.

Trips were arranged to Salisbury for special occasions. These included the Royal Visit in 1947 (the Queen actually spoke a few words to my brother during this; what a day!), and visits by the English and Australian cricket touring teams which were making tours of South Africa and Southern Rhodesia. I saw both Len Hutton and Ray Lindwall play in these matches. The top forms also went to see Lawrence Olivier in the films of 'Hamlet' and 'Henry the Fifth'. And in my final year we all listened to the broadcast of the marriage of Princess Elizabeth to Prince Philip.

Each year by tradition the first eleven played a cricket match against a team from Government House. In my final year the school eleven was the best for a decade, and its captain made a century in this match, with some help from the Governor's team captain. When Jimmy Leggatt was in the nineties and still not out, the umpire called time, to be informed that his watch was fast, that the Governor's watch was the only one which could be correct in Rhodesia, and it showed there to be ten minutes of play remaining. This imperious intervention provided sufficient overs to be bowled to enable Jimmy's century to be reached - no mean achievement for a thirteen year old schoolboy it was considered.

At school I lived in modern buildings equipped with electricity, proper sanitation and piped water. When I went home I returned to a more primitive way of living. We had no electricity, so no electric lighting, cooking or refrigeration facilities. We had no telephone; our lighting came from paraffin lamps or candles. The bathroom I have already described; we had no piped water. My brother and I often used the same bath water. The lavatory, or P.K. as it was known (short for Picccanniny Kia - 'little house' in Chilalapa) was a long drop earth closet enclosed within a round hut with thatched walls and roof which stood some thirty yards away from the main house. It was cool and well ventilated. A Paradise Flycatcher suspended its beautifully woven nest from a branch near it one year, and reared its young regardless of the regularly passing human traffic. The male bird helped incubate the chicks, its long rufous tail dangling over the edge of the nest as it did so. The round walls of the lavatory meant that there was a half- moon of floor behind the seat; my mother discovered a cobra coiled up there one day, much to the amusement of her sons. Night visits meant that one took a hurricane lamp. This I regarded as inadequate for seeing if leopards were prowling round it in search of young boys to eat, so my nocturnal visits were made as quickly as possible.

Our radio was powered by a car battery, which had to be taken to Rusape once a fortnight to be charged, or my mother would miss her favourite BBC programmes.

I went about on the farm dressed only in shorts and a shirt for most of the year and I often went barefoot about the house. Walks required shoes to protect one's feet from thorns, and I habitually wore 'tackies', the Rhodesian name for canvas shoes with rubber soles. These were very useful when climbing rocks. I went up these like a rock rabbit without thinking, often leaving the dogs unable to follow me. It was only on my return to the farm many years later that I realized just how steep and dangerous some of these rocks were. The Victoria Falls hotel had a dress code posted on that visit to Zimbabwe. "Dress - Smart Casual - No Tackies, No Tee- Shirts" it read, and I at once felt back in familiar territory.

My favourite item of dress was my Baden Powell hat. After seeing too many cowboy films I decided it would be much improved with a bullet hole through it. So I 'borrowed' Dad's .303 rifle one morning and took both into a secluded part of the bush behind the house. There I placed the hat on top of a handy rock, took careful aim with the rifle and pulled the trigger. The hat disappeared, and the rifle kicked me, severely bruising my lip. The result when I recovered the hat was disappointing. I had hoped to find a dramatic neat round hole in it with blackened edges, but the effect of the bullet on the hat was barely noticeable. The felt had simply closed up behind the bullet leaving no sign of enemy action. I quietly replaced the rifle, and sympathetic enquiries at lunch later that day concerning the cause of my swollen lip were met with a non- committal mumble.

For most of the year when it was warm I slept on the verandah. For a while one of the Irish Terriers would also sleep on my bed but I discouraged this when my brother told me that leopards often took dogs at night. The idea of a dog being snatched from off my feet was not to be thought about - what if the leopard made a mistake? Thereafter I was in the habit for a time of putting a lethal weapon such as a catapult or an airgun beside my bed at night so that I could protect myself. These formidable weapons would not have frightened the smallest leopard, but they were reassuring to me.

I had a mosquito net over my bed during the rainy season. We once had a delightful pet, a bush baby.

These were soft-furred little galagoes, with large eyes, ears which folded flat and prehensile hands. They slept all day, awoke at nightfall, and their favourite food was chocolate. They delighted small boys by their ability to climb up their own tails. Tiddles, as our bush baby was christened, would nightly come climbing over my mosquito net chittering and begging to be let in so he could play. He was about as big as my two hands put together. I would allow him in and have games with him, tickling and wrestling him with one hand to his and my great joy. When I became sleepy I would put him outside the net, and after patrolling round it for a while he would retire into the night to hunt for beetles and moths. After I went back to school he disappeared for ever. I hope he found a mate.

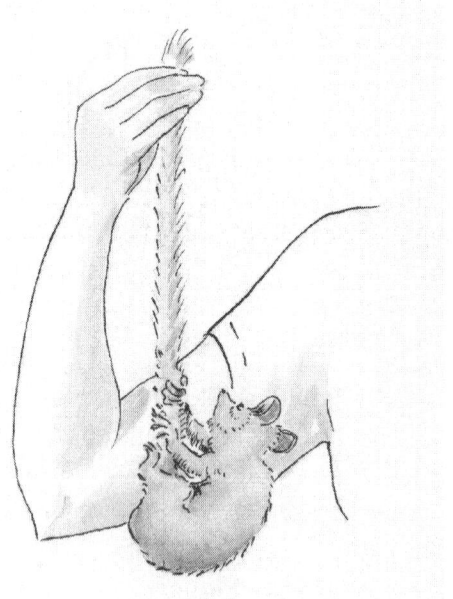

Bush baby climbing its' own tail.

Chapter 22. Stuck down a hole

Kopjies provided us boys with many and varied adventures. Among their numerous inhabitants were 'daasies', or rock rabbits. These little animals were not real rabbits but hyraxes; they were called rock rabbits by the English and daasies by the South Africans. They lived in crevices high up in the rocks, from where they would peer down and chitter at the dogs, disappearing rapidly into their holes when humans came too close to them. Their chittering incensed the dogs, who occasionally tried to follow them down their holes. We had one foolish little terrier who got stuck doing this one day. It was quite impossible to reach her or to dig her out, but after endless calling and yelling she eventually managed to extricate herself.

Rock rabbit family.

The terrier's experience should have been a lesson to me, but young boys seem to think they are immortal.

In addition to many of the kopjies having been fortified by the Mashona in the past, they had also been used as places to bury their dead. It had been their custom to lay the bodies of their relatives in crevices in the rocks and to wall them in with dry stone walls. With the bodies they often placed the worldly possessions of the deceased. Wild animals in course of time demolished the walls, and we boys were quite used to seeing human skulls and bones scattered around. With them among the rocks could be found clay pots, beads made from ostrich shell, bracelets made from brass wire, and even rusty spear heads and old bows and arrows. Such finds we regarded as archaeological treasure, and we had no compunction in hunting for and collecting it. What boy could resist picking up a genuine bow, or an arrow with a lethal arrow head?

One hot day, alone with the dogs, I found a promising looking little cavity in the rocks in a part of the big kopjie we rarely visited, because it was so steep and overgrown. The cave sloped downward into darkness, and I thought looked worth exploration. Into it I crawled, and soon found that not only did it slope downwards, but that it became narrower and shallower as it did so. I was eventually reduced to crawling down into the increasing darkness on my stomach, with both arms stretched out in front of me. I went as far as I dared, but not having a torch and finding nothing but daasie dung and dust around me, I decided to make my way out.

But, Oh Lord! I now found when I tried that I could not go back! My belt buckle had become hooked over a pointed spur of granite on the floor of the cave which, when I tried to wriggle backwards, held me fast like a fish on a hook. Worse, I could not get my hands back to undo the buckle, since my arms were pinned in front of me by the rock walls and roof of the cave, which prevented me from drawing them back. I might be there yet if I had not been wearing a Boy Scout belt. The round buckle end of this threaded through a metal slot in the opposite end, and was then twisted to keep it in place. My desperate wriggling eventually made the round buckle twist and then slip back through the slot to release me, and I shot out backwards, dusty, dirty, and not a little relieved to see daylight once more.

"Wuff!" panted the little Irish terrier bitch, jumping up as I came out and panting with the heat, "we wondered if you were stuck".

"Well", I said to myself, "would you dogs have waited around, if I hadn't been able to get out? Because I doubt if anyone could have found me down there otherwise."

Chapter 23. Wild Life and Birds

There was none of the big game, which tourists to game reserves in the lower and drier parts of Rhodesia still expect to see, left in our district. Elephant, lion, giraffe, buffalo, sable, even the delicate oribi once common around Rusape, all were long gone, although the Bushmen had left a record of them in their paintings on rocks and caves all round us. But there were still many other wild animals and exotic birds, and from time to time we had a glimpse of the rarer of them.

One hot still morning we climbed the big kopjie at the bottom of the farm; its dominating presence seemed more menacing than usual. The air felt oppressive; the dogs were less active, they panted, and their tongues lolled in the heat as we toiled up. On reaching the summit we rested awhile near a pile of huge boulders which marked the summit at one end. There were cracks and fissures in these rocks, hiding caves and crannies under, in which rock rabbits lived. These little animals usually chattered a warning when we got near, but there were none to be seen that day. Once rested, we rose to set off homeward, but we had only gone a few steps when the whole kopjie suddenly twitched, then heaved. There was a crashing noise as boulders, disturbed by the earthquake, for such it was, went rolling down the sides of the kopjie, bouncing off rocks and trees as they went. Shaken, we stood for a second, not yet realizing what had happened, when out onto the boulders near us bounded a caracal, the African Lynx. It had been lying hidden in one of the caves underneath until frightened out by the earth shaking around it. There it stood, in its reddish coat, the fur on its tail standing out like that of a cat treed by dogs. It turned its head, snarled, and with a lithe bound was gone. Wordlessly we turned and hurried down the steep slope, picking our way between the fallen rocks. For the rest of that day I felt nauseous , and my mother had a head ache, consequences of the earthquake we both thought. It was only later that we realized what a rare sight we had been given. Caracals are not common, and no one had seen one in our area before. But we had seen it quite close to us on the open rock, both of us had seen it, we could not have been mistaken.

On the far side of these same rocks there was a cave between two of the biggest boulders, around which was an open platform. This rocky perch provided a superb panoramic view of both the farm and the district round it, so was a favourite destination. There was only one approach to the platform, since there was a sheer drop on every other side. On my own one day, armed only with a .22 rifle, I was scrambling over the rocks to reach it when I saw a movement inside the cave. I stopped, and there, silhouetted against the open sky at the back of the cave, was the unmistakeable profile of a leopard. It was trapped; there was no other way out of the cave except straight past me. I made a hasty retreat; a small .22 rifle was no weapon with which to try and stop a leopard. I went back to that platform many times afterwards, the last occasion with my son nearly forty years later. Each time I did so, I always had a very careful look to make sure the cave was not occupied before climbing over the last few rocks.

In the middle of the kopjie, on the highest pinnacle, the farm beacon had been built. Above this, in the sky on a cloudless spring day, we once saw a great black eagle with chestnut back and stubby tail, stooping, climbing, twisting and rolling in ecstatic aerial acrobatics. This was a Bateleur Eagle (bateleur is the word for an acrobat or tumbler in French) , performing his mating ritual for his prospective wife. My brother, sadly, was not present to see this; as a keen ornithologist, he would have been even more delighted than we were.

We had a pet duiker for a while. Its mother had been caught in a snare laid by an African, leaving the young fawn to be discovered an orphan beside its dead parent. Cissie brought it back to the farm and reared it on a bottle. I remember it butting imperiously against the back of my bare legs when it was waiting its turn to suck , just as bottle fed lambs do. Pittipat, as she was named, was as delicate as a ballerina, and seemed as vain about her appearance as one when she grew up. She came onto the house verandah from time to time, but gave this up once she discovered how undignified she looked there when her elegant little black hooves shot from under her on the smooth concrete floor and she performed the splits. She left her name to posterity, as my mother wrote an illustrated short story for children about her.

Pittypat the duiker, admiring a portrait of her ancestors.

Baboons were the animals I disliked most; I found them very frightening. They moved around together in tightly knit packs, with young males acting as sentries. The shouted barks of " Wahoo! " by the sentries gave advance notice to the rest of the pack whenever danger appeared, such as the appearance of a white man or a leopard, and would be repeated by the rest of the pack. (Leopards were known to prey on them). But small boys they regarded with contempt. Each pack would be led by a fearsome old male with front teeth as long as my index finger; they could tear a pursuing dog to pieces as they would hold it down with their hands as they bit it Often they acted as a pack to protect a wounded member. My brother was charged once when he shot one.

Dead crop stealer.

They had an intelligence which was almost human. One evening I was sitting quietly at the base of the big kopjie, well hidden and waiting for them. I could hear them preparing to settle down for the night. The young ones were squealing and romping around like naughty children, totally disregarding the grumpy grunts from their elders. Suddenly one exasperated mother seized a disobedient youngster and there was the unmistakeable sound of a slapping, followed by indignant wails. It was so like human behavior that it was eerie.

They were the great enemy of farmer, as a pack could do terrible damage to a crop in a very short space of time. An African told me that when a baboon went into a maize crop, it tore off the first maize cob to hand and tucked it under one arm. It would then go to the next plant, tear off the cob and tuck that one under its arm, dislodging the first. It would then proceed up the row, repeating the procedure until the entire row was picked. This story was related with a great deal of gestures, and much laughter. I suspect it was a fable rather like some of the Kalulu stories, rather than the truth. The baboon damage I recall was far less tidy.

Chapter 24. Snakes and Ladders

Although there were many changes in the colony after the second world war, life did not become much easier for my parents on the farm. My mother's life had been focussed on her children, but with my brother and I now both at boarding schools we were away for eight months of the year, during which time she was alone on the farm with my father. New neighbours had appeared in the district, a few of whom became good friends, but there were none who were interested in literature, poetry or painting, the subjects dear to her heart. The nearest village, unlovely Headlands, which had hitherto consisted of not much more than a railway station, a police station, Baron's Stores and a hotel which made most of its income from its bar, now had a village hall, in which amateur dramatics were performed. I can recall seeing a Ben Travers farce in which my mother took part with great gusto. But tennis parties remained the common social activity, and whereas she welcomed the opportunity to meet people, she was getting a little too old for tennis, and she found the main subjects of conversation, which revolved mainly round labour problems, recipes, and babies among the women, and round the weather, labour problems, tobacco prices and the failings of the government among the men, rather boring.

Restarting farming at the age of fifty, particularly after having spent the last part of the war beside the Red Sea, where the climate was hot and unhealthy and there was no social life, cannot have been easy for my father, particularly as many of those who had continued to farm in his absence had prospered. As so often, farmers had made money during the war when prices had risen and imports had been restricted. Money was also being made by tobacco farmers after it, since Britain did not wish to import tobacco from America, from whence it had to be paid for in U.S. dollars, and so was importing it from the colony. But my father lacked the capital which was required to build the barns in which tobacco was cured. Doubtless the capital could have been borrowed, but he hated borrowing. He did however, acquire some modern equipment. A small Farmall Cub tractor, which had to be started on petrol and, once it had warmed up, then ran on kerosene, made its appearance, but the wonderful little grey Ferguson tractor with its innovative hydraulics, which became so popular in England, was unknown to us.

More useful was a Chevrolet fifteen hundred-weight pickup. This was a tough American made vehicle with the ground clearance and suspension essential on the rough roads in Africa. Its gear change was on the steering column rather than the floor, and the brake was placed on the right of the driver. These factors, together with a bench front seat, allowed three to sit side by side in front. I learnt to drive in it, having first driven the little tractor.

A new dam was built at the bottom end of the farm after another dire drought and a new borehole was sunk in the same area. This had a pump driven by a diesel engine in a little pump house; like most of its ilk, the diesel engine was a devil to start.

The main source of the farm income came from the eucalyptus plantation which had been planted in the nineteen thirties. The trees from this plantation provided the long straight poles for telegraph poles and also the tier poles in tobacco barns on which tobacco leaves were hung to cure.

My father did not make life easier for himself since he would not delegate work. To be fair, unlike those who had continued to farm throughout the war, he had not had time to train staff, and the increase in the number of farmers after the war made it more difficult to recruit good labour. Africans started to come down from Nyasaland to seek work; they were pleasant people, but language difficulties and the short term nature of their contracts meant they needed constant supervision.

Being conscientious, my father worked hard and long. He was up and about long before the rest of his family, rising at half past five every morning. As a result, he was constantly tired, which made him reluctant to leave the farm. Two people left alone in such circumstances, with different interests and outlooks on how life should be lived inevitably get on each other's nerves, and arguments flared from time to time. I found these painful, and I would disappear in misery after hearing them.

My mother for a while took a job as a school matron in Salisbury. This enabled her to be at home for the school holidays. But it was very hard on my father, left by himself on the farm. We did not have a trained African cook, and I am sure his diet suffered.

Lastly, both my parents were worried about my elder brother. He did not find life at school easy, not having either great ability at games, which would have provided easy popularity, or exceptional scholastic capability, although he was quite capable enough to obtain a place in Natal University when he left. His great interest was in birds, but that did not then offer the prospect of a career. Meanwhile his younger brother was doing better at his school, usually nearer the top of his form than the bottom, and winning prizes for English and History. All this, combined with the problems of adolescence, meant that Kenneth was unhappy at school. I do think he was bullied - he certainly never confided to me that he had been - but he became a bit of a 'loner', and for a while there was a distance between him and my father.

Children can be self centred, and with two thirds of my time being spent at boarding school, I was involved in my own struggle to survive, or escaping life with my nose in a book, while all this was going on. But grownups now started asking me the dreadful question, "What are you going to do when you leave school?" As I supposed I had at least six more years to spend at school, this seemed a very premature enquiry. Nevertheless, I found in the school library a book which had a profound influence on me. This was the autobiography of Kingsley Fairbridge, who had spent much of his boyhood in Rhodesia, but in a very different time to the one I knew. He was born in South Africa in 1885, and in 1896 his father, a surveyor, was offered work in Rhodesia. His young son, who had already started to help his father with his surveying calculations, joined him there, travelling by ox wagon from Beira to Umtali to do so. Life in the barely settled colony was rough and uncomfortable, and the young boy soon started to say he did not like it. His father offered him a choice, either stay and work, or go back to Grahamstown, and school. Kingsley decided he would stay. Within two years he was helping his father to survey the route for the new railway line from Beira to Salisbury, and was building survey beacons on the tops of kopjies, many of them near Rusape.

"A lad of thirteen, dressed in shorts and shirtsleeves, I walked on the outskirts of the Empire," he wrote, "I saw the dust blow from the rising embankments...fig, and thorn and kaffir orange vanished before the axes... the stone kopjies were rent with dynamite that the bridges of the British might be established in security. And so I went ahead on the tide of progress, thinking of the thousand homesteads that would someday dot these plains..."

I was entranced. This had happened only fifty years ago, and only a few miles away. I even knew the names of the kopjies on which he had built beacons.

At the age of fifteen, Fairbridge was given the opportunity to accompany an acquaintance on a journey on foot to the Zambezi. Early on the way the friend fell ill, but, undaunted, Fairbridge went on alone , accompanied by one African and a rifle. To reach the Zambezi he had to cross some of the wildest and least inhabited parts of the country. But reach the Zambezi he did. On the return journey, often hungry, he contracted malaria. It was at this time that he reached an ambition to bring disadvantaged children from the cities of England to Rhodesia to give them the opportunity of a new life in the colony. In one of his poems he wrote,

"I looked, and beheld...

The brown of the veldt, the unending immensity

League after league, houseless and homeless, a country

Abandoned to emptiness, yearning for people."

To achieve his ambition he decided he should go to Oxford University, to educate himself and to meet those who would be in a position to help him. Now with a goal in view, he in due course won a Rhodes scholarship to Oxford. Once there, he decided that a 'Blue' would help him. He chose boxing, learnt to box from scratch, and eventually won his 'Blue', defeating on his way one Julian Grenfell, the golden boy of the age notorious for writing the poem "Into Battle", and perishing shortly thereafter on the Western Front.

The immediate effect on me was not to give me the incentive to go to England to further my education for an ideal, nor to take up surveying as a future career, both of which events took place later, but to make me take more interest in boxing. A knobbly little man with a broken nose taught this at Ruzawi once a week; his name was Mr. Agiotis, and he was known to us as 'Aggie'. He had a farm near the school and was popular with us since he allowed us to fish in a dam on his farm on Sundays. I believe he had been a fly weight champion in South Africa before he retired to Rhodesia. He taught the basics of stance, footwork, guard and jab in boxing, and refereed three round bouts during which we boxed with opponents of similar weight. For the whole of one winter term, instead of kicking a football around during morning break, I hammered a punch ball, and at the end of term I won my weight in the end-of -term competition. I never learnt Fairbridge's 'trick of the heavy punch' so, alas, could never win my bouts with one mighty blow as he did, but I earned the respect of other boys, and became more confident in myself as a result.

Encouragement in another sphere came from a good teacher. Mr Taylor had retired from a position at a public school in England and, undaunted by his age, came out to Rhodesia to teach us Latin. At this he was very good.

I found myself in the upper fifth form, and then in the sixth, both of which had only ten pupils. These small classes enabled us to receive intensive teaching, and, thanks to the efforts of Mr Taylor and others, I astonished everyone by winning a scholarship to a major public school in South Africa.. This school was St. Andrew's, in Grahamstown, one of only four schools in South Africa privileged to select a Rhodes scholar for Oxford, and coincidently, where Kingsley Fairbridge had spent time.

And so I left Ruzawi. Returning home that day I was allowed to drive my mother and I all the fifty miles home in the Chevrolet pick-up. I was not yet fourteen and had no driving license, but I felt very proud and grown up.

Chapter 25. A long railway journey.

To reach my new school, St. Andrew's College in Grahamstown, I had to go by train. This journey took four days and three nights, with changes of train at Bulawayo, near the Rhodesian border, and Alicedale in South Africa. There were a number of public boarding schools in Grahamstown for both boys and girls, and a special train was provided to take pupils from Rhodesia there and back three times a year. So we spent three weeks each year travelling to and from school. There was a special concessionary fare for this privilege, which was £5-13s. Four days on a slow train through large areas of hot arid country proved boring, even for avid readers like myself, and bored children are often mischievous. I do not know if special guards were put on these trains, but I do know that no member of staff from St. Andrews ever accompanied us.

Between Plumtree, the last station in Rhodesia and Palapye, the next stop in Bechuanaland (now Botswana) white- uniformed Customs Officers joined the train and inspected passports. Progress through this dry low-lying land was slow, and as the temperature rose the train went slower. On some of the long uphill gradients it was a pastime for some boys to leap off the train from the front coach, run beside the carriages as they passed, and to catch the last coach by jumping onto the steps leading up to the open platform at the rear. The consequences of not catching the last coach as it passed could have been serious, but I do not remember that anyone ever missed it.

At Palapye the steam train gasped to a halt at midday, and took on more water for its boiler. Beside the scruffy platform buildings a circle of concrete had been laid, and while the train refilled its water tanks, a small wind- up gramophone was brought out, and passengers would get out and dance to the scratchy notes of a record. At this halt another treat awaited. Vendors sold water melons. A quick whip round in the compartment would provide the necessary shilling to buy a whole melon, a welcome source of wet and sticky refreshment. Each compartment held six passengers. At night four bunks would be let down to provide sleeping tiers on each side, and a bedding roll of blanket, sheets and pillow provided for each occupant.

The next major stop was Kimberly, where Cecil Rhodes and Alfred Beit had made their fortunes, (the Alfred Beit Trust had provided the buildings, built in the Dutch Colonial style, at Ruzawi). Kimberly itself was an ugly city, only memorable for 'the Great Hole' formed during the diamond- mining excavations, and its acres of shanty slums. I found South African attitudes to Africans repellent; every seat on every railway platform bore a sign, 'Slegs vir Blanks' (Seats for Whites).

I eventually arrived at Grahamstown tired and dirty, to receive another shock. As a scholarship boy, last minute accommodation had had to be found for me, and instead of being in one of the regular Houses, I was to live with three other boys with the Headmaster's secretary. She was an impecunious widow, and was not very welcoming. I suspect we were there as paying guests, and as a means of increasing her income. Worse still the four of us were members of Day House, that for non- boarders at the College, most of whom lived with their parents in town, and who were a despised minority to the rest of the school. Adding to my isolation, I was English, spoke no Africaans, and had never played rugby, the national game in South Africa. Finally, I was now once more at the bottom of the heap as a new boy, but found myself two forms above most of my contemporaries, since Ruzawi had educated its pupils to a much higher standard than many equivalent schools in South Africa.

St. Andrews had a reputation as one of the top four Public Schools in South Africa, but I was not happy there, and have few fond memories of it. I can recall only one teacher whom I liked, an English teacher who wrote in my school report that she hoped I would one day publish something.

It also had a Sea Cadet Corps. I joined this because the idea of 'parade ground bashing' with the army cadets did not appeal to me At the end of one term the Sea Cadets were put on a South African frigate, the S.A.S Transvaal, which took us from Port Elizabeth to Durban. During that voyage I was very seasick, and was hit by a flying fish when polishing the brasswork of a Pom- Pom gun on the upper deck. I did not find this naval experience a stimulating one; it certainly did not point me towards a future naval career.

Meanwhile my brother Kenneth was also undergoing his trials and tribulations in South Africa. On leaving school he had obtained a place at the University of Natal to study Forestry. There he found that the tone of the university was very South African, and that although tuition and exams were all in English, his lack of ability to speak Africaans and to excel in sport made him an outsider. He was also continually short of money, although he was certainly not a spendthrift. I don't think my parents had any idea of how much money he should have had on top of his basic tuition and accommodation fees, and this cannot have helped. A plan was discussed of sending him to Edinburgh University after he had completed a year at Natal, but he became very depressed, and after only a few months he applied for a place at the Rhodesian Forestry School at M'tao, where the students worked as they learnt, and received a small salary. He was accepted, and gave up his University place, to the disappointment of both my parents.

I must have been conscious of the unhappiness this uncertainty about his future had caused, but buried my head in books when at school to avoid it. I started to read books about the Royal Navy. Two authors took my fancy - both wrote under pseudo-names - 'Taffrail', and 'Bartimaeus'. Quite how these books found their way into a South African School library I cannot think, but they contained stories about gallant officers at the time when the Royal Navy was at the height of its pride which quite carried me away, and to the utter astonishment of my parents I suddenly told them I wanted to join the Royal Navy. As I was of the right age to apply for entry to the Britannia Royal Naval College at Dartmouth, I then found myself faced with the prospect of entrance examinations to that establishment.

I was by this time preparing for Matriculation exams at St. Andrews, and was fourth or fifth in my class, so rather arrogantly thought that preparation for the Dartmouth exams was unnecessary. Whether a syllabus was ever sent to St. Andrews I do not know, but all went well in the solitary room set up for my Dartmouth exams until I opened the English Literature paper. I normally reckoned I could pass any English Literature paper with ease, but my heart sank when I opened this one. I discovered that a list of ten books on which I would be questioned should have been given to me well beforehand so that I could study them. But I had no recollection of seeing this list. The paper contained ten questions, one on each book, and required me to answer five. Of the ten books in the reading list, I had only a passing acquaintance with five, but certainly not to examination level. The first question I saw that I knew anything about concerned Shakespeare's 'Julius Caesar'. This play had been put on one winter term at Ruzawi, and I had taken a very minor part in it. It had been produced by Mr Taylor, and such had been the enthusiasm and vigour of his rehearsals that I retained sufficient memory of it to give a passable answer. Another book on the list was Robinson Crusoe. I had read a children's version of this at some time, so at least had some knowledge of the plot. I ground my way through the rest of the paper, duly answering five questions. Fate must have been on my side, for in due course I heard that I had passed the written Dartmouth entry examinations, and scrutiny of the results showed that I had received the minimum pass mark in English Literature – 50%.

I next had to pass an interview. It was not possible to take the quite rigorous tests that prospective cadets underwent in England, and a special interview was set up for me in the Royal Naval base at Simonstown, near Cape Town. This required yet another long train journey. I have a vague memory of a Captain and two Commanders interviewing me: they appeared sympathetic, possibly being impressed by the distance I had come alone to attend. I was successful at the interview, and after medical and eye tests, suddenly found I had been accepted as a Royal Naval Cadet.

For the rest of my last term at St. Andrews, I worked very little, and I left with few regrets. Meanwhile my parents were digesting this bombshell which I had presented to them. They received a telegram of congratulation from the Governor of Southern Rhodesia, no less, and after that there was no question but that I had to go. A passage was booked for me on the Athlone Castle from Capetown to Southampton, and contact was made with my uncle in England, who agreed to look after me until term started at Dartmouth. All too soon I found myself saying farewell to beloved dogs and shattered parents, and making an even longer train journey to Simonstown, where the Royal Navy had agreed to accommodate me in a frigate until the Athlone Castle departed for England. I shared a cabin in the frigate with a Midshipman doing his National Service. He was having the time of his life; Simonstown was one of the most popular ports in which a Royal Naval ship could be based, and he spent most of his free time ashore at parties with gorgeous girls. He had one girlfriend in particular, who seemed most accommodating; he called her 'the White Rabbit'. When I asked why he replied airily, "...because she has very little between the ears". It was all very educational to someone as innocent as I, and did nothing to discourage me from my naval future.

My education continued in the Athlone Castle, an ancient liner which shuddered continuously, its main engines were so worn. I shared a second class cabin, where the bathing facilities used salt water straight from the sea. I washed my hair in this with soap one night, to find that soap in salt water turns to a sort of glue, which is very difficult to remove. At the end of the cruise there was a Fancy Dress Ball. Not knowing what to wear, I unwisely took the advice of some older girls, who promptly dressed me in their own clothes as a girl. I still looked very young and had no need to shave, and I found to my horror that I was accepted as a girl and required to dance as such; an obviously short sighted man started to make passes at me while I was trying to do so. I think he was even more shocked than I was when he discovered his mistake.

I landed in England in early April The country between Southampton and London seemed bleak, and not as green as I expected. At Waterloo I was met by my uncle Christopher's wife Jeannette, and precipitated into a whirlpool of activity. I was taken to Gieves in Bond Street to be measured for my cadet's uniform, made from the best doe-skin cloth. I was taken to the Tower of London. I went skating with Camilla, Jeannette's young ballet student daughter, and left humiliated as I constantly crashed to the ice while she twirled gracefully round me laughing. I was taken to the visitor's gallery of the House of Commons by Christopher, who was a distinguished parliamentary consultant who knew his way round the House better than most M.P.s, and from there I saw a debate on a Transport Bill in which was apparently being conducted, "the biggest filibuster in Parliamentary history". During this debate a hunched Winston Churchill wandered in surrounded by cigar smoke, took a casual glance around the Chamber , and decided the fuss did not require his presence further. In all too short a time I found myself, "self-conscious but proud" , in my cadet's uniform on the train to Dartmouth, where on arrival I was pitched into a whirl of activity even more hectic than that before.

The Royal Naval College then was rather like a public school, but one with a unique character of its own. When I joined, cadets entered at the age of sixteen, and left at eighteen to join a training ship. There was still a civilian teaching staff, some of whom left to teach at Westminster or Eton when the entry system changed after I left, who taught academic subjects such as English, French, Mathematics, Mechanics, Physics, etc. History was taught with an emphasis on the importance of British sea power. In addition we learnt navigation, seamanship, and engineering. Something had to make way for the latter three subjects, so there was no Latin, although there had been a Latin paper in the entrance examination. The cricket and rugby teams played local public schools such as Blundell's and Sherborne.

Cadets slept in 'chest flats' rather than dormitories. Each cadet had a sea chest at the bottom of his bunk, on which his kit had to be laid out nightly in a time honoured and immaculate manner. 'Rounds' were made every evening to inspect these. 'Late turnouts' were occasionally awarded for an especially tidy chest, punishments for the opposite. Canings could be given by Cadet Captains, who were the equivalent of prefects at a public school. The White Ensign was raised and lowered with ceremony daily. All cadets were issued with a bosun's pipe on a lanyard; daily routine was governed by bugle calls, or pipe calls made by duty cadets. Each cadet also had a 'hussif' containing needles, thread, etc., and a heavy seaman's knife with a marlin spike on it. No cadet was allowed to hold more than ten shillings. We were paid four shillings a week. This did not go far, as we had to buy our own boot polish, which was consumed rapidly with all the shining we had to give our shoes. The first of many parades which we attended was to receive pay. This harked back to the time when, once 'the king's shilling' had been accepted, the receiver inextricably became a member of the service. Everything we did was carried out at 'the double'; we doubled between classes, we doubled to meals, we doubled (cursing as we did so) up the myriad steep steps from the river to the College, down which we had already doubled to learn small boat handling or sailing. We ate our meals in a panelled dining hall surrounded by portraits of famous admirals, being encouraged to consume second helpings by Miss Buller, the ex-Wren Catering Officer whom few would ever forget. It was the policy to rush cadets off their feet during their first term; we rose at six forty in the morning, took a cold bath, and went exhausted to our bunks in the evening. I had little time to think of Africa.

My first letter to my parents from the College ended, "…I am feeling rather small, lost and homesick, but I'll soon get over it, I expect."

I did, but I think now this gave my mother her final excuse to return to England for the first time since she left it in 1929. She was to be there when my first leave became due.

Chapter 26. Tragedies.

In June the Coronation took place. Older cadets were sent to line the processional route or march in the procession; the rest were given leave. I stayed with my uncle, who obtained places for his daughter Camilla and myself in the United Services Club, from which we could watch the procession, and then the ceremony on television. He and Jeannette had seats outside the Abbey. I think Camilla and I had the best of it, as it poured all day. Soon after the Queen reviewed her Fleet at Spithead from the Royal Yacht; all cadets attended the Review, being accommodated in the hangar of an ancient aircraft carrier. These events provided welcome breaks during my first hectic term at Dartmouth, at the end of which I went 'ashore', on leave.

My mother arrived in time for this and to meet old friends and family. The friends included her former landlady in London, Miss Byrne, who had survived the Blitz in her house in Notting Hill and who was still taking paying guests, and Nancy Gee, who had a small flat in Chelsea. Then we went down to Cornwall to stay with Phil Wailes, her beloved Aunt Flo's son. A new life began for both of us. We had the warmest of welcomes, were accepted into the family, and enjoyed the happiest of summers. Every evening we played games which I am sure had not changed since Cissie had left for Africa - drawing games, consequences, penny novelettes, etc. My mother's skill with a pencil and her robust sense of humour provided new zest to these, and she blossomed. For myself there was tennis to be played with Phil's daughter Joey and other cousins, swimming and surfing at Mawgan Porth, walks along the coast, and visits to the Falcon Inn in St. Mawgan, where Phil, regardless of my age, introduced me to beer. He was the first adult who had ever treated me and discussed things with me as an equal. He read widely, and was happy to talk about books to me and to introduce me to new writers. I would never have read 'Zen and the Art of Motor Cycle Maintenance' without his enthusiastic recommendation. My horizons began to widen. The many visitors welcomed into Marver House at all hours were a wide and catholic lot, varying from well-known archaologists and professors down to the postman and 'Sarge', a cockney odd-job man who had settled in Cornwall after service in the the Duke of Cornwall's Light Infantry in the First World War. Sarge liked young people, and often regaled us with lurid tales:- "...seventeen on me baynit, and then it broke..." was one memorable quote which left young Andrew with his mouth open, and the rest of us helpless with laughter. The idea of Sarge, who was only five foot and a bit tall, with seventeen of the enemy spitted on his bayonet like a kebab was outrageous.

I went back to Dartmouth and my mother stayed on in England for several months. She made several visits to a dentist - those in Rhodesia being mostly of indifferent quality, and seldom visited because they were too far away- but I think this provided her with an excuse to delay her departure from her newly rediscovered cousins and happiness.

But her presence was missed. My brother had been having a tough time. He had joined the Rhodesian Forestry Service with about a dozen others of his own age, some of whom were pretty wild. They were supposed to learn 'on the job', but were used as cheap labour, and were often sent to the wilder and less attractive parts of the country, where they lived rough in tents, or poor accommodation, without proper catering or sanitary facilities. Some Forest Officers put in charge of them found them a nuisance, and so get rid of them to places where, if they caused trouble, no one would hear of it. A combination of the bad water, unhealthy climate, poor diet and the tropical diseases prevalent in these areas is not a recipe for good health, and Kenneth, normally as fit as most young men in the country, began to suffer from various tropical complaints. Not surprisingly, he once more became depressed about his future, but found no-one to confide in. My father was becoming lonely and withdrawn coping on his own, and Kenneth found that, when he went back to the farm, it was no longer as welcoming a home as it had once been. He wrote sad letters to his mother, telling her that it was impossible for her to continue to live on the farm, and that my father should give up farming. About this time my father was offered a job near Marandellas, and hearing this, I plucked up courage and wrote to encourage him to do so. But nothing came of it, so I assume the offer was turned down. Then my brother left the forestry service, and took a job with a private company growing wattle trees in Inyanga, a decision which his father did not like.

My mother eventually set sail for Rhodesia in the S. S. Uganda after Christmas. Kenneth's health continued to deteriorate; by the time my mother left England he had had treatment for tick fever, followed by injections for bilharzia, a debilitating disease caught from a parasitical worm found in contaminated water. This treatment, he wrote, made him feel even worse than he had felt before it.

Before my mother reached home she received a telegram on board ship to say that Kenneth had been killed in a motoring accident.

The accident occurred following a bilharzia injection he received from a doctor at a nearby Mission Station. Whether the accident happened as the result of the after effects of the injection is conjecture, but the motorbike he was riding crashed into a Landrover driven by another young man employed by the wattle company.

My parents were both devastated. My father had to deal with the funeral all on his own.

"... at the funeral it broke my heart to see Maurice standing there so solitary but so controlled - only once did he come close to losing that control...", wrote a friendly neighbour after it..

And it was a terrible homecoming for my mother, who arrived too late to attend, particularly as she felt all might have been prevented if she had returned earlier.

I received the news from the College chaplain and a last letter from my brother two days later. Sadly, in that he wrote of his desire to go to England to obtain better qualifications - a wish which had it been fulfilled would have changed his life for the better. I felt helpless being so far away at such a time; there was nothing I could do but carry on.In the summer of 1954 my parents paid for me to fly home, and I returned to spend what were to be my last weeks on the farm. Once back, I was happy to fall back into to my old way of life, wandering the bush clad in shirts and shorts carrying my father's rifle, absorbing the unforgettable smell of Africa, and listening to the Cape Turtle doves calling distantly through the sunshine: -

"Where's father? Where's father..."

The faithful Irish terriers accompanied me, so happy to have me back.

During this holiday the opportunity for me to talk to my father about the possibility of his giving up farming never seemed to occur. In fact this was because I did not have the courage to raise the subject. I was aware that my father was set in his ways and that it was difficult for him to accept that he should abandon something which he had built up over so long, and with so much hard work. I was only just eighteen, and I felt I was still too young to do so. Furthermore, it was a subject which I knew would be likely to start, once again, an old and never to be resolved argument, at a time when I knew both my parents were still in mourning for my brother. I regret this now as I know my mother wished me to do so, but I still consider that it would have not changed events.

On my last night we had dinner together in a hotel in Salisbury. We had wine, and I saw my father in a new light, quiet and courteous as ever, but charming as well. No wonder my mother had fallen in love with him in earlier days.

And so I returned to Dartmouth. That term we went to sea for a week in a frigate. During that cruise Cadet Greenhow was instructed during a practical navigation instruction to "take a bearing on that lighthouse", to which he unwisely replied, "what Lighthouse?" All was discovered; I had been becoming short- sighted for several terms before the discovery was eventually made. I had first noticed it when my shooting on the rifle range deteriorated, due to the fact that I could no longer see the bull's eye of the target clearly. And at the beginning of each term all cadets were given an eye test, as Naval Officers in the Executive Branch were required to have first class sight. Failing to read the bottom line of the chart earlier, I had memorized the letters while numerous cadets after me recited it aloud, and the authorities had never changed the chart. But by now I was finding it difficult to read anything on a blackboard in class, even when sitting in the front row, and the discovery was inevitable. There was a fuss; I was sent to a specialist in Harley Street for an opinion; I came out with a prescription for glasses. The glasses transformed my vision of the world, but the result was inevitable; if I wished to remain in the Royal Navy, I would have to become a Supply Officer. Meanwhile there were examinations to be passed and greater responsibilities to be taken on in my final term.

All this, together with the usual pace of life at the Royal Naval College meant that I did not focus sufficiently on other things going on outside my own frenetic little world. One which was apparent was the increasingly depressed tone of my father's letters; I did write to tell my mother about this.

I finally 'passed out' of the College tenth in my term and collected the Prize for English, which gave me great satisfaction after my difficulties with the entrance examination in that subject, and went on leave to stay with my aunt Jeannette, unaware of what was to come. When I got there I was told by Jeannette that my father had committed suicide.

Chapter 27 My mother returns home

What followed must have been some of the worst few weeks of my mother's life. The discovery of my father's body- he had shot himself with his army revolver which the Army had so inefficiently allowed him to retain after the war - then living alone on the farm and clearing up, all the time with the feeling that she had been in part responsible for my father's death. It must have been dreadful.

My father was buried in Rusape graveyard beside his son Kenneth.

The farm was sold in haste. Consequently, it fetched at auction only £2600. To those who think fortunes were easily extorted from the colonies, the original purchase price was £1706 13s 5d. The latter price was for bare land, completely undeveloped. Since buying it in 1921 my father had cleared three hundred acres of land for ploughing, fenced boundaries and paddocks for livestock, built two farmhouses, cow sheds and other buildings (mostly with his own hands) and installed a cattle dip, a well, a windmill, a borehole and water pumps. He had also planted seventy acres of eucalyptus. The timber from these trees was sold separately, and fetched £6800, more than twice the price received for the farm. However, a dispute subsequently arose between the purchaser of the farm and the timber buyer, which eventually led to the trustees of my father's estate having to compensate the former. I still think it was mean of the new owner to extort money from a widow, by then in England, for the timber feller's actions subsequent to the farm sale.

With hindsight, things could have turned out worse if my father had lived on and continued farming on Chigwani. After his death my mother was able to return to England before Ian Smith's Declaration of Independence and the war which followed in Rhodesia. Had my father still been farming while that war went on, he would have been in the thick of it. The farm was not far from the mountainous border with Mozambique, where most of the guerrillas were based, and they made many of their incursions past it. They ambushed a bus carrying Africans on the main road only a mile away, just below the Ship Rock which my brother and I used to climb as boys . They may even have machine- gunned many of the Africans in that bus from that very vantage point. The neighbouring farm, which I visited many years later, was by then surrounded by a high security fence, erected during the war to protect the occupiers, and will have been confiscated from its owners without compensation since. One of the daughters of the Staceys, my mother's neighbours and close friends during the Second World War, was shot dead in her car with her children beside her when driving in a convoy going to South Africa. I remember her playing Titania in 'A Mid Summer's Night Dream'. Zimbabwe at the time of writing cannot even afford to hold its own internal elections and is requesting foreign aid to do so. And instead of exporting food to large parts of Africa as it used to do, it is now unable to feed its own people. I am told there are now only two fully - productive farms on the main Salisbury to Umtali road which ran past our farmhouse. That road used to serve one of the most productive farming areas of the country, with farms along its whole length. Zimbabwe is now a very sad place.

My mother returned to England as quickly as she could. Her cousin Phil helped her find a house in St Mawgan, only a mile or so from where he lived. Ironically, this house was purchased for the same price that Chigwani Farm had fetched in Rhodesia the previous year.

In due course she was able to recover and settle down. Through her cousins she made new friends and started a new life. She continued with her water colours, and made graphic cartoons of village cricket matches and fetes. She made woodcut covers for the church magazine, went brass rubbing and joined the Womens Institute. She took part in their Dramatic Productions in which she acted, or for which she made inspired costumes out of old clothes and scraps.

In due course she enjoyed having her grand - children to stay, making them delightful birthday and Christmas cards every year with illustrations and poems by herself.

A Birthday Card for her grand-daughter.

After leaving the Royal Naval College, I went on to become an Officer in the Supply and Secretariat Branch. I served on an air station, and in ships in Scotland and the Mediterranean. I saw active service during the infamous Suez crisis when I was a Midshipman in H.M.S. Jamaica.

The Supply Branch was responsible for mundane matters like naval stores, catering, pay and accounts, ship's correspondence and returns, and secret documents. When I joined the navy I had intended to be an Executive Officer, and after a few years as a Supply Officer I decided that the bureaucratic work in an office below decks required by that department was not for me, despite the compensation of foreign travel. So I resigned my commission while I still had time to take up another career. I qualified as a Chartered Land Agent and became a resident land agent on a big estate in Devon. This made another major change in my life, which I have never regretted since. It also made it possible for me to be closer to my relatives in Cornwall.

I have returned to Zimbabwe, as Southern Rhodesia is now called, several times and have revisited my father's old farm, now in African occupation. I climbed to the summit of Ruanda once more, accompanied by my son. The eucalyptus trees planted by my father were still there, a landmark of an Imperial past and visible from miles away. Baboons, remaining in residence, gave angry barks of annoyance at my reappearance. I remembered each rock, cleft, tree and cave on it; the mimosa trees at its base still flourished. The kopjie seemed to have grown steeper and more difficult to climb than when I had last done so in 1954. Was this was because it was the end of the wet season, when everything was still lush, and the blackjacks and creepers clutched at my ankles as I fought my way up, or was it that, now in my in my fifties I was no longer as fit as I had been when a cadet at Dartmouth? What had not changed was its dour outlook. Ruanda still spreads its menace like a dark shadow over the land beneath it and will still do so when all men are dust.

From there I went on to see the graves of Kenneth and my father in the graveyard outside Rusape, both well - tended I was relieved to find. Finally, I called on June Searson , daughter of Daphne, with whom Cissie had stayed prior to her marriage to my father. June was still living in her grandfather's house. The only change made to it since my mother had left it for her wedding in 1930 was a security grill erected on the outside of the verandah to protect the house during the war for independence.

If you are born in Africa you are left with a feeling for Africa in your bloodstream. Why this is so I cannot say: it does not have the softer and subtler charms of England. But England too has a hold on its children, and England always remained 'home' to my mother.